Return to Childhood
The Memoir of a
Modern Moroccan Woman

Modern Middle East
Literatures in Translation
Series

Return to Childhood

The Memoir of a
Modern Moroccan Woman

by

Leila Abouzeid

Translated from the Arabic
by the author, with
Heather Logan Taylor

The Center for Middle Eastern Studies
The University of Texas at Austin

Library of Congress Catalogue Card Number: 98-075404
ISBN: 0-292-70490-9

Printed in the United States of America

Cover design: Diane Watts
Series editor: Annes McCann-Baker

Published in Arabic as *Ruju 'Ila Tufula*
by Leila Abouzeid, Rabat, 1993

Foreword

The publication of Leila Abouzeid's *Return to Childhood* signals a new development in her work, a shift from fiction to nonfiction, but more specifically to autobiography, a genre little validated in Arabic literature of the past. But this situation has begun to change, as Abouzeid discusses in her introduction written especially for the English edition. *Return to Childhood*, like her novel, *Year of the Elephant*, is a richly textured chronicle based on memory: memory of a tumultuous period in the history of Morocco, the last days of French colonial rule in the early 1950s and the emergence of the independent nation state in 1956. The events of the time form the background of this autobiographical work, a landscape which Abouzeid peoples with remarkable men and women, their troubles and triumphs, their humor, and despair. For she writes about the people caught up in the historic events, particularly women, and she is concerned with how family relationships shift and sometimes break in a time of radical social and political change. Since this is a personal memoir, the author's focus is her family, whose fortunes reflect the conflicts of the period: her father was a recognized hero in the nationalist struggle; her illiterate mother had to manage alone with four daughters and meager resources, and often was forced to move.

Abouzeid's narrative invites the reader to share in the dilemmas of the men and women who, whether they wished it or not, were carried along in the swirl of anti-colonial demonstrations and revolutionary ideals. The reader views those dilemmas from the private world of the family, with its secrets and conflicts. We follow the course of the nationalist movement from its beginnings to the year 1953, when the French exiled the sultan. This turned out to be a tactical error, since the exiled sultan then became a martyr-hero of his people. We see the child Leila with her mother and sisters, bringing food to the prison where her father has been incarcerated by the French for his anti-colonial activities. We hear Leila's mother arguing with her old aunt about the little girls' future: should they be sent to the new schools, as their father insists, even from his jail cell; or should they be apprenticed to learn the marketable skill of making caftan buttons? Moroccan Independence was declared in 1956 and the sultan returned in triumph to be hailed as King Mohammed V.

But, the narrative does not end with the joyous days of Independence. It goes on to chronicle the complexities of its aftermath and the struggle for power between the new monarchical government and those resistance figures associated with the opposition party, the Union Nationale des Forces Populaires (UNFP). Leila Abouzeid's father once

i

more becomes a dissident and is imprisoned again, this time by his own countrymen. It is after this point that we hear, in the narrative, the adult Leila questioning her father about his political strategies and criticizing his treatment of her mother.

Return to Childhood is narrated in the voices of three generations of women: Leila's mother, her grandmother and herself. As one of the reviewers wrote of the Arabic edition, she has "given voice to the voiceless women of old Morocco. We see the men only through the eyes of women." These three women's voices tell us about the old world of the medina, the traditional city, with its tales of local scandals and family disputes, its humor and superstition and herbal medicines; we see that world's collision with the emerging world of political uprising, public education, and modern medicine.

The memoir raises difficult questions about the consequences of violence, the shape of the new nation, the limits of personal as well as public responsibility. Many of these questions remain unresolved at the end of the autobiographical account, which is of course the case in everyday life. As it unfolds, Abouzeid's narrative of childhood assumes broader meaning and acts as a literary, metaphorical statement of how change affects ordinary people everywhere.

First published in Arabic in 1993, the memoir was a best seller in Morocco. The author states that choosing to write her autobiography in Arabic, her mother tongue, rather than in French, the language of the colonizer, was for her a political act. That choice may have been a risky and limiting act in 1990s Morocco, where Arabic as a literary language had not received as much acceptance among intellectuals as might have been expected, given the post-independence euphoria of the 1950s and 1960s, which included a strong national educational program of Arabicization. But Abouzeid, who is also fluent in French, insists she is willing to take whatever risks are involved, in order to build a local Arabic readership for contemporary North African literature. In this effort, she joins a select group of Tunisian, Algerian, and Moroccan writers who continue to publish in Arabic.

Elizabeth Warnock Fernea

Author's Preface

Autobiography, until the last few years, was not respected as a form in Morocco. For Arabs, literature meant the lyric, the poetic, and the fantastic, whereas autobiography deals with the practice of daily life and tends to be written in common speech. As late as the fifties, Khalila Bennouna, the first Moroccan woman to publish a novel, in the fifties said of the Moroccan writer Rafiqat Attabi'a that she was not *adiba* (a literary woman writer), because she could not write fiction but wrote about the realities of her own life.

Autobiography was not classified as literature because it was also thought to be accessible to all; after all, the thinking goes that everyone can write about his or her life. Statesmen have done it, as well as artists, especially those in earlier times, who are seen as mere entertainers who ended up as artists because they could not succeed in a real career.

In addition, autobiography has the pejorative connotation in Arabic of *madihu nafsihi wa muzakkiha* (he or she who praises and recommends him- or herself). This phrase denotes all sorts of defects in a person or a writer: selfishness versus altruism, individualism versus the spirit of the group, arrogance versus modesty. That is why Arabs usually refer to themselves in formal speech in the third person plural, to avoid the use of the embarrassing "I." In autobiography, of course, one uses "I" frequently.

Perhaps even more important, a Muslim's private life is considered an *'awra* (an intimate part of the body), and *sitr* (concealing it) is imperative. As the Qu'ran says, *Allah amara bissitr* (God ordered the concealing of that which is shameful and embarrassing). Hence, the importance of *hijab* and *hajaba* or *yahjubu*, from the root "to hide," words used for the veil that hides a woman's body and the screen that hides private quarters as in the Qur'anic verse that says *Kallimuhunna min warai hijab* (Talk to them behind a screen), referring to the wives of the Prophet. The word for the ancient Arabo-Islamic walled city, *muhassana*, is the same as the term for chaste unmarried women; it means literally "inaccessible." The concern about concealing is clear in Arabo-Islamic architecture, where inner courtyards and gardens are central, windows look inward rather than outward, and outside walls are blind.

In the forties a man sued his neighbor in Sefrou to stop him from building a second floor and he won the case. The irrefutable argument was that the neighbor was going to have access to the man's family's intimacy because he would overlook their courtyard. Autobiography allows everyone to overlook one's private courtyard.

Autobiography must be seen then as an imported genre in modern Arabic literature. It was introduced in Morocco in the 1950s by Ahmed

Sefrioui with his childhood narrative, written in French, *La boite à Merveilles* (The Wonder Box). Similar works, also in French, may be seen in Paul Bowles' series of records and translated Moroccan autobiographies: these include Mohammed Chukri's *Bread Alone* and later Abdelhaq Serhane's *Mesouda*. The only Moroccan childhood memoir written in Arabic is *Fi Attufula* (In Childhood) by Abdelmajid Benjelloun, which is set not in Morocco but in Manchester, England, where the author grew up.

For me, writing an autobiography was therefore even more unusual, because I am a woman, and women in my culture do not speak in public, let alone speak about their private lives in public. When I published my first article in a Moroccan newspaper in 1962, I did not even sign it with my real name, but used the pseudonym of Aziza, and when I published my first novel, *Am al Fil*, in 1983, I left the protagonist's home town unnamed because it was my own.

In other words, I had to wait twenty-eight years before I dared write my autobiography, and I did it in response to a request from my friend Elizabeth Fernea. The work was meant for a non-Moroccan audience, and I felt it would give me the opportunity to correct some American stereotypes about Muslim women.

I wanted to say that, yes, I am a Muslim woman but I am perfectly capable of taking up the pen to present my own perspective about my country's reality. And, the translation of *Am al Fil* into English (*Year of the Elephant*) did clarify some misunderstandings about Islam and Muslim women. As Michael Hall from the University of Melbourne, Australia, stated:

> The sheikh in the work, like the text of *Year of the Elephant* itself, stands in sharp contrast to the lurid images of "mad ayatollahs" and "fanatical fundamentalists" all too common in Western media and academic discourse alike .... In many references throughout the text Abouzeid reinforces an essentially positive image of Islam as a force for social change and liberation. It is of course unlikely that she set out to challenge negative Western stereotypes about Islam when she wrote *Year of the Elephant*, as the novel was written for an Arabo-Islamic readership who does not share Western prejudices and misconceptions regarding Islamic religion and culture. Once translated into English, however, the text presents an immediate challenge to Western discourse on Islam, opening the question of the role and value of translation within the field of postcolonial literature.

An American reader told me, "I thought that Morocco was the Morocco of Paul Bowles, meaning the underground Morocco of hashish addicts and outcasts." This was "the Morocco of 1912" as a Moroccan critic put it.

For these reasons I wrote *Ruju 'Ila Tufula (Return to Childhood)* in Arabic and did a rough translation of it into English. Elizabeth Fernea had asked me for a piece of fifteen to thirty pages to be included in an anthology of childhood narratives from the Middle East. At first, I thought that I would not have enough material, for my childhood did not seem to be a source of inspiration. But when I started, memories came back so quickly that I was amazed by their abundance and clarity. The process lasted two months, during which I filled enough pages for a book. When I went back to those pages, I discovered something else. These pages seemed to be of value, and I said to myself, "Why not publish them in Arabic as well?" I called a Lebanese publisher, who answered, "If only they were Brigitte Bardot's." But he confirmed my belief that they might appeal to an Arab audience.

And there was another problem. Since the autobiography had been written for a foreign audience in a sharp tone and in total frankness, I was apprehensive about the reactions of many people, including particularly my family. I put the manuscript away and forgot about it for over two years. When it was finally published in Casablanca in 1993, my family did not only approve but were very enthusiastic. Moroccan readers and critics also received it with enthusiasm. Mohammed Chakir, a respected, young critic in Morocco, classified it as an autobiographical novel because he found features of the novel in it, "multiplicity of voices, nonlinear narration, description, atmosphere, mood, and the poetic."

Other reviewers said things like: "*Ruju 'Ila Tufula* is bold and courageous"; "its criticism of both the system and the opposition is by far more daring than that of any of the male writers who are active members of the opposition parties"; "Abouzeid is a woman's writer in Morocco, par excellence"; "her female characters are voices rather than images and bodies as they always are in male writings"; and "*Ruju 'Ila Tufula* gives credit to oral history, an oral history told by traditional, illiterate women."

Since 1993, four autobiographies have been published in Morocco, two of them by women: *Dreams of Trespass* by Fatima Mernissi and *Ma Vie, Mon Cri (My Life, My Scream)* by Rachida Yacoubi.

Elizabeth Fernea was still considering the possibility of including in her anthology only fifteen pages abridged from my much longer English manuscript, but when she looked through it she thought that the entire text would be worth publishing as a separate book. Heather

Taylor, who took the photograph for the cover design of *Year of the Elephant* (University of Texas Center for Middle Eastern Studies edition), graciously agreed to edit the rough draft of my own English translation of the childhood memoir. She has warm feelings for my country and said she was excited by the project. She worked on it with sincere good will, despite other commitments.

I am convinced that the quality of the translation of my autobiography is due to Heather Taylor's editorial skill, and her particular care and concern to render my text accurately, clearly, and creatively. I am thankful to Elizabeth Fernea for helping to make the publication of this translation possible and for having entrusted its editing to Heather Taylor. I hope that this memoir of my childhood will find as many readers as *Year of the Elephant*.

Leila Abouzeid

Chapter I
EL KSIBA

The intercity bus pulled up and stopped. It stood in the road that links Fez to Marrakech, opposite the El Ksiba sign at the corner of a smaller road that ascends the Middle Atlas mountains. We got off and the driver's assistant brought our luggage down from the roof. The bus resumed its journey. We crossed the road, going toward the sign. My mother sat down on the ground, and put Naima on her lap. Fatiha sat next to her while my youngest uncle, Sidi Mohammed, lifted the pieces of our luggage and placed them in front of her.

We were on our way back home to El Ksiba after one of our trips to Sefrou, my mother's hometown. As usual, she was returning loaded with brass cooking pots, wooden washing basins, wood trays, braziers, and short brooms. She would say, when she was in a good mood, "I buy useful things to have near me when I need them." She was convinced that in El Ksiba she was living in the wilderness. But when she was upset, she would criticize herself and say, "Smart women buy gold, but I buy pots."

A truck appeared on the main road from the opposite direction and turned toward El Ksiba. My uncle waved and walked over to it while my mother shouted, "Say you are Si Hmed Bouzid's brother-in-law."

The driver stopped and looked down. "I only have one place," he said. "The truck is full."

"Nobody else but me needs a lift," said my uncle. "I want to go to El Ksiba to tell my brother-in-law, Si Hmed Bouzid, that we've arrived."

"Get in, then," said the driver.

My uncle walked around the truck and climbed into the passenger's seat. The truck began to move. The sound of its engine changed, grew faint, and finally faded away. Silence prevailed, a mountain silence offset by the cry of a sheep and a distant voice answering a call in Berber. Refreshed by the mountain air, I left my mother and sisters by the El Ksiba sign and wandered along the side of the road beside the wild *boubal*, with its soft yellow corn wrapped in leaves. I remember the peace of that place, for, of course, I did not know then what that day was to bring to my family.

We were three girls with our mother by that sign that day, and if Khadija had not been dead we would have been four. Khadija had died of measles in Rabat, where we had lived for eight months, and where my father had been working for the *Nasara* (Christians) – the word generally used by Moroccans to refer to the French colonists. During our stay in Rabat, his employers had allowed him to study at the Institut

1

des Hautes Etudes, located in the green-domed building that now harbors the Moroccan Faculté des Lettres et des Sciences Humaines. We had lived in one of two apartments on the ground floor of a building across the road from Moulay Youssef Hospital. Our next-door neighbors were Jmia and her husband, a black Moroccan couple. They shared their apartment with a poor French family whose father was a caretaker in the nearby Christian graveyard. Every time my mother sent me on an errand to Jmia, I found the French woman sitting on a chair in the courtyard in front of her room mending socks, with a sewing basket on a table in front of her. I cannot remember her in any other way. In contrast, my image of Jmia is that of a slim, tall, very black woman wearing a Moroccan dress with her head wrapped in a scarf. That was the apartment where Khadija died and Naima was born. Khadija died before she could talk. She was probably no more than two years old. Once when she got lost a policeman asked her, "Who are you?"

"Me," she replied.

"And who is your father?"

"Daddy," she answered.

One day soon after Khadija died, my father came home and found my mother crying. "What's the matter?" he asked.

"It's Jmia," she answered. "Here I have lost my baby and that woman still puts rouge on her cheeks."

"Suppose she does, who's going to see it anyway?" he retorted.

My mother told that story with a smile every time she spoke of Jmia and always concluded it this way: "She was a great neighbor, may God bless her soul if she is dead and mention her with good words if she is alive. She stood by me at the time of Khadija's death, but I wish that she had not put rouge on her cheeks."

Did I think of Khadija that day, by that road sign? I am certain I did, because it had become my habit to say, "If Khadija had not died, she'd be with us now," or "If Khadija had not died, she'd be three now." I had not forgotten her and still haven't. To this day, every time I drive by La'lou graveyard where we buried her I look at the gate and say, "May God bless your soul, Khadija."

Only a few days ago I had Naima's two daughters with me, and I slowed the car down and told them, "See that gate there? To the right is the grave of a little sister we had. Her name was Khadija. She died the same year your mother was born. Ask God to bless her soul."

Sarrah asked. "Why?"

"Because He answers children's prayers."

"Why?"

"Because He loves them."

And if I still remember her now, I must have thought of her that day, by that road sign, less than a year after her death.

We heard a bus coming. It made a turn toward El Ksiba, reached the sign and stopped. The driver's assistant jumped down and came over to my mother. He squatted beside her and told her something. She began slapping her thighs and rubbing her palms together and saying in a tragic tone, "Oh my empty house! Oh my mother!"

The man said, "Stay here until I return. I'm going with the mail to El Ksiba and I'll be right back." He got on the bus by the back door. It resumed its monotonous roar and disappeared up the road.

Then my mother told us, "The Nasara have put your father in prison. Not because he did anything bad, but because he is a nationalist. 'Nationalist' means someone who wants the Nasara to get out of our country, and that's honorable." But her moaning disturbed me much more than the news. Still, her distress made it difficult not to think of prison as something bad.

In El Ksiba, where we lived after leaving Rabat, certain inmates of the local prison were assigned to us by the French administration to do errands in the village. Those prisoners had been arrested for minor infractions of the law; most had injured somebody or stolen something. One had been arrested because he did not salute the French contrôleur général when he passed him on the street. One day, while still serving his sentence, he was taking the dough for our bread to the village bakery when he met the same Frenchman, riding his horse. He put the breadboard on the ground and saluted him with both hands. The Frenchman asked, "Two salutes? Why?"

"One is for you and one is for the horse," answered the inmate.

Every time my mother heard that story she would say, "The poor man must have told himself, 'If he could put me in jail because I did not salute him, he might increase my punishment if I don't salute his horse.'" Then she would add, in a sad tone, "It is the law of the powerful. The law of the jungle."

And now, I thought, she says that jail is honorable! When the bus returned, Belaid, the driver's assistant, helped us get on and we went back in the direction from which we had just come. At Zaouit Cheikh, we got off and Belaid took us to his house, but we soon left it and took another bus to my father's hometown, Beni Mellal. There we found my paternal grandfather's house crowded with people. Some of them began to cry when they saw us, and my grandmother started beating her breast.

Then my uncle Sidi Mohammed entered carrying a brass candlestick and my mother asked, "What's that?"

"That's all they left you. It was behind a door and they did not see it."

She said, "Who do you mean, 'they'?"

"Your father-in-law and his son Ma'ti."

"Oh no!" she cried.

"Yes," he answered.

That day marked the beginning of our troubles, which my mother would describe in detail over and over again, to the end of her days. But her perceptions were different from mine, for I was a child.

In the rooms of my paternal grandfather's house in Beni Mellal there were Bedouin blankets, rugs and mats, earthen pots and jars, and trunks and looms. My grandfather, Hammadi Bouzid, was always sitting in the courtyard with a brass tea tray in front of him and a wooden sugar box next to him.

In contrast, in my maternal grandfather's house in the city of Sefrou there were banquettes, cushions stuffed with wool, pillows in velvet cases bordered with silk trimming, fine curtains, beds, carved wooden cabinets, storage spaces and shelves displaying antique Fez bowls. At that fine house they mocked my father's family. They said, "Meat is all they eat." "One whole cone of sugar a day." "All they care for is their stomachs and penises," implying that all the men of my father's family were interested only in eating and having sex.

But at my paternal grandfather's house, they mocked my mother's family for their excessive concern with material things. They said, "City dwellers live surrounded by tiles and marble, and they are avaricious and stingy. Their possessions are so dear to their hearts that there is not a thing that costs money for which they would not affectionately use the diminutive form — they even say, 'the little egg, the little bread.' And they are reluctant to part with anything." Then my grandfather would add, "As for me, sir, I will eat and drink whatever I like, no matter what the cost, for tomorrow I may die."

Every time my grandfather said that, he followed it with his story about the Fassi, the merchant from Fez, which he told while leaning on a large pillow in the courtyard. "My friends and I went to Fez and bought all our merchandise from that Fassi, and afterward he invited us to lunch. So we went. We got to his house and found that it had a really impressive door, and inside were tiles up to the ceiling and carvings and pillars. There were mattresses stuffed with wool so high that one needed help to climb up and sit on them, and also velvet and embroidered cushions. So, anyway, the Fassi clapped his hands and a black maid came with the hand-washing basin and kettle; then she placed the table in front of us and brought the food. It was only some salads and some bowls of ground meat and eggs. When we left we were still hungry. So I stopped, sir, by the butcher, bought a leg of lamb, took it to the caravansary and cut it up myself, and my friends made a charcoal fire and we grilled the meat and had a real lunch."

Another thing I remember from that day at my paternal grandfather's house in Beni Mellal, in addition to the crowd and the crying, was Kabboura, the sister of my paternal Uncle Said's wife. On that day Kabboura insulted my mother. I had heard that my paternal grandmother had wanted my father to marry Kabboura, but when he refused and married my mother instead, Kabboura married his best friend Driss, a carpenter who played the lute. After Kabboura revealed her animosity toward my mother that day in my grandfather's house, my mother would often compliment herself when she thought of Kabboura, saying, "She should be grateful to me! I'm the one who taught her how to conserve peppers and cook lemon chicken."

The next thing I remember from that visit is that my mother, my sisters, my maternal uncle Bouazza, and I were in a room locked from the inside, and a huge woman, not Kabboura, was banging on the iron work of the window. Still another strong image is my mother, my sisters, my uncle, and I sitting by a thorny hedge surrounding an orchard opposite my grandfather's house, and my cousin Aicha, who was my age, watching us with contempt from the doorway, eating a slice of melon and then throwing the rind toward the hedge.

El Ksiba is the diminutive of Al Kasaba (the citadel), the Arab name for a Berber village in the heart of the Middle Atlas. One gets there from the Tadla Plain after a difficult drive past houses built of plastered earth, situated among oak trees and oleanders growing along the sides of a little river. After seven kilometers, the road splits in two. One fork goes to the village; the other has a low white wall along the road that in the years before Independence marked the entrance to the administrative quarter where the French worked and lived in luxurious mansions. Moroccan soldiers' families also lived in that quarter, in more modest houses, all alike, inside the whitewashed walls of a fort. The walls also enclosed two larger, better houses for the two Moroccan civil servants employed by the French. For a time, we lived in one of these houses.

Past the fort was the administration building, followed by the Frenchmen's houses, all in a row. Then the road went on up to the village of Imilchil, running parallel to the river and through what was then a summer resort reserved for the French. The village center lay two kilometers from the administrative quarter beyond a small pine forest, past the administration's vegetable and fruit garden, past the school and the hospital.

It was to the administrative quarter that my uncle, Sidi Mohammed, had gone that day to inform my father of our arrival. My father, Ahmed Bouzid, worked as an interpreter for the Berber people and for the French. I do not know how he learned Berber, because he was from Beni Mellal, which is an Arab town. The name is a distortion of Beni Hillal, the name of the primitive Bedouin tribe that achieved fame by migrating from Arabia to North Africa in the twelfth century. The historian Ibn-Khaldun was referring to the Beni Hillal's reputation as destroyer of cities when he wrote his well known words: "Whenever something is arabicized, it is destroyed."

My father's family was notable for its social status, not its wealth. A Bedouin's social status was traditionally determined by his ability to consume and offer food, not by his possessions, and those practices resulted in the dissipation of the family's financial resources. Besides, the necessity to be always on the move prevented the Bedouin from amassing many possessions and from leaving any permanent architectural heritage.

My paternal grandfather, Hammadi Bouzid, was a well-traveled tradesman, but he was not rich. Surprisingly, however, he owned his own house. He had two wives, the younger of whom was my father's mother, Khadija. She was a gorgeous fair-skinned Berber. My grandfather had brought her home from one of his business trips. However, as soon as I became aware of things around me, it became clear to me that she spoke Arabic with a local accent, and nothing about her denoted her Berber origin except her fair skin and the tattoos on her cheeks. So she could not possibly have been the one who had taught Berber to my father.

My father had entered school by order of the central government, and was the only educated member of his family. This is how my mother told the story: "The local district officer came and took him. He was the eldest of his mother's three children, the one who looked most like her and the one whom she preferred. People said in those days, 'The Nasara are going to teach their language to our children and turn them to their religion.' Women advised her to give him an herb to make him have a fever when they came to take him."

"But what happened to those who refused to send their children to school?" I asked.

"They went to prison."

So my grandmother had given my father that herb and carried him on her back, covering him so he would sweat, and his face would turn red. But they came and took him anyway.

My father was smart, but the French authorities allowed him to study only until he finished primary school. Then they appointed him as an interpreter in the town of Moulay Ali Shrif, far away. There he met Driss, the carpenter of the French administration. My father admired the life of city girls and asked Driss to find him a wife in his hometown, the city of Sefrou. The result of this search was Driss' sister-in-law Fatma—or Fettouma, as she was called—my mother. It is extraordinary that a family in Sefrou would even consider such a match, because that town had a refined Andalusian culture, and its people, like all people of Andalusian origin, were known for their chauvinism. They hated outsiders and would never marry their daughters to them, especially if they were Berbers or country people. Yes, my father was educated and yes, he had a good position, but he was an outsider and a country man. The reason they agreed to permit their daughter to marry him was that she was already divorced and had a baby girl. Later, whenever my father brought her trouble and unhappiness she would say, "May God punish him who matched me with you." She meant Driss, of course, my Aunt Khnata's husband.

My father married my mother and took her to live in Moulay Ali Shrif, but he soon was transferred to El Ksiba and they moved there. As time went by she would often say, "He was a good man in Moulay Ali Shrif, the land of *baraka* (grace, blessing) and prayer, where women could not be seen anywhere and when you did see them they were covered from head to foot as in Hijaz. But he changed when he came here to this den of vice that does not know God."

Our house in El Ksiba included four rooms and a central courtyard; the walls were covered with grape vines. My mother told us that when her father planted the first vine he predicted, "When someone eats the fruit of this vine he will say, 'Bless the planter.'"

There were beds of mint on each side of the entrance to the courtyard and a water fountain at the end of it. Buckets were filled with water from this basin to purify the threshold of the front door of the house. This practice had become necessary after my mother came back from Sefrou with her father one day and found some evidence of witchcraft buried on the threshold. She was cleaning the house, bent over her short broom. When she got to the front door she saw that the threshold was broken. She swept away the earth and then kept digging with the end of the broom handle until she found a row of reeds underneath. Under the reeds was an animal's flat shoulder bone with Hebrew writing on it. She called her father and sent for her husband at the office. A great commotion followed, with my mother crying. My grandfather took the bone down to the village rabbi, who told him that it had been inscribed and buried under the threshold in order to separate Fatma, daughter of Fatma, and Ahmed, son of Khadija. These were the names of my parents and grandparents.

It was a sinister day. I felt gloomy and fearful. I don't know how old I could have been, but I remember the flat bone being passed from one hand to another. I remember the hole, the earth, the reeds and my mother in her checked apron, with tucked-up sleeves and a tied head scarf, gesturing nervously and speaking loudly, and my grandfather's turban and short white beard. After that, I began to scream in my sleep at nights.

Another image from that house is associated with a strong odor. This image is of two big, black, dead birds in a cabinet that was probably under a sink, because the memory of the smell hints of humidity.

There is also the memory of the pine woods outside the fort where we played. Fatiha, Khadija, and I were minded by one of the prison inmates when we played by the brook. The air was thick with the smell of spearmint, which grew on both sides of the water and mingled with the scent of pine and resin.

In that place were tiny Berber orchards surrounded by dry thorny hedges. They looked like "patches" or "handkerchiefs," as a French geography instructor was later to call these plots of agricultural land in Morocco. Inside each of the hedges was a plastered earth house, chickens, a tethered cow, and pomegranate and orange trees. The oranges were yellowish with fine, soft, skin and tasted different from regular oranges.

A school stood at the edge of the pine woods, a school with two classrooms and a red-tiled roof. I spent a few months there learning the French alphabet and some elementary grammar.

Once through the classroom window I glanced outside at a green meadow where a yellow cow gleamed in the daylight. I remember well how this view, framed by the window, suddenly became a fixed image that sent my mind astray. I had a deep sense of some unseen omnipotent force behind the image and was seized by a dazed feeling of mystery. And there is an image mingled with feelings of loathing and resentment, that of the hat worn by French officers, with its visor and gilded brocade decoration.

In El Ksiba village we lived for awhile in a house with one of those tiny Berber orchards. There we had a watchdog named Rabbah. He was stolen by mountain peasants from the weekly market. He stayed with them for three months. Then one day he followed them to the market and eventually returned to us. I remember the feeling of joy and other emotions that arose in me as he pushed the orchard gate open and entered, emaciated and exhausted from the journey, his fur covered with red dust. I was moved by his faithfulness and the way he had apparently tricked his kidnappers so that he could come back to us.

And there is another memory of a large basket slipping into the waters of Oum-Errabia and being swept away by the current. On top of the basket was a white blanket woven in the style of Sefrou . We stood under the bridge at the entrance to the town of Tadla pointing at it, and followed it with our eyes, crying out, "It's gone! It's gone!" Our mother, dressed in her djellaba and her face veil, stood there, beating the back of her left hand with her right hand, saying, "Oh my empty house, it's gone!" But I cannot remember what we were really doing under that bridge.

I have an image of a parcel that we opened in the courtyard, and in it we found wooden dolls wearing caftans and belts, their heads wrapped in scarves secured tightly by patterned strips. The dolls' faces had round eyes and mouths drawn in black on white cloth. A few months later my maternal grandmother, who had mailed those dolls to us, arrived with my grandfather, my uncles Bouazza and Sidi Mohammed and my unmarried aunts Zhor and Hachmia. They all planned to stay a month with us. I waited for one full day before I said to my grandmother, after dinner, "Tell us what has been happening in Sefrou."

She listed the marriages that had taken place there, describing each one in detail, telling us about the upholstery, the number of cushions and blankets, the amount of the dowry, the bride's and groom's presents.

Then my mother asked her, "Has anyone died?"

My grandmother mentioned those who had, offering reasons for the death in each case. Then she announced, "Zineb's husband Mohammed has gotten out of jail and left town."

My mother commented, "He lost face and could not confront people."

My grandmother continued, "After he got out of jail he went to his father-in-law and told him, 'I have done what was written in my destiny, and now I am determined to leave this town. I don't know what's in store for me, and I don't want to involve your daughter in my punishment. So, if you want me to divorce her, I will.' His father-in-law replied, 'I am a Muslim who bears witness that there is no God but God and that Mohammed is His Messenger. I am neither a Jew nor a Christian and I will never tell you to divorce. Take your wife with you, my son, and let what happens to you happen to her.'"

"What a man!" said my mother, shaking her head and clicking her tongue in admiration.

"He made the less damaging choice," my grandmother observed. "He chose estrangement and loneliness for his daughter rather than divorce. May God preserve our daughters and the daughters of all Muslims from it."

"Grandma!" I interrupted. "Tell us about how he picked up the safe and carried it downstairs all by himself!"

"And where did he go?" asked my mother, ignoring my intrusion into the conversation.

"They say to Rabat."

"Zineb is unlucky, like me," said my mother. "Providence has also thrown *her* into estrangement and loneliness."

"Grandma," I persisted. "Tell the story from the beginning, from when they were like brothers."

"I have told it to you all a hundred times."

"But tell it one more time."

She smiled and straightened the folds of her caftan and said, "Well, pray for the Prophet."

"May God's prayer and peace be upon Him," we responded.

Then she began: "Mohammed and the Shrif (a descendant of the Prophet), Moulay Hfid, were friends. They shared everything that was permitted by religion and were like blood brothers. Moulay Hfid trusted his friend with his family and possessions. He was rich, whereas Mohammed was a mere tradesman. The Shrif did not let anyone else see his wife, but he let Mohammed see her and let him enter his house whether he was there or not. Time passed. The Shrif had a safe in his house, and Mohammed had taken note of this.

"One year, during Ramadan, it became the habit of the two friends to eat dinner at home and meet at the café and stay there until *suhur*, the last meal before sunrise. But when Mohammed decided to betray his friend, he came to him and said, 'They say that there is a new movie in Fez. Don't expect me in the café this evening. I'm going to Fez to see it.'

"And the Shrif said 'All right.'

"Mohammed ate dinner at home, then looked in the café to make sure that the Shrif was there, and then proceeded to his house. The house was being repaired and there were scaffolding posts in the alley. It was a private alleyway for the Shrif's family. They were rich, I tell you.

"When Mohammed reached the house he said to the Shrif's wife, 'When Moulay Hfid comes, tell him that I went to Fez.' Then he slammed the front door from the inside, took off his shoes quietly, and went upstairs to the room where the safe was. He remained there until the lights went off and the wife, her children, and the maid all went to sleep.

Then he carried the safe out to the gallery overlooking the courtyard. He went downstairs and brought in a scaffolding post, laid it on the staircase, put the safe on it and slid it down until he got it to the entrance. Nobody knows how he took it from there back to his own house."

My mother suggested, "Maybe he had a cart. It must have been a cart."

"A cart or something. Only God knows. So, he took the safe. He had in his house a sort of garage and below it, down a staircase, a cellar full of wood and iron, which he had previously moved aside. He hid the safe there and piled the wood and scraps of iron on top of it and then went to bed."

"How could he?" commented my mother.

"When the Shrif came home he ate his *suhur* meal and went to sleep upstairs so that he would wake up late and not be disturbed by the children. He found the room open and the safe missing.

"He called his wife and asked, 'How has this happened?' and she said, 'I don't know.' They found the door leading to the roof open. Mohammed had opened it to make it appear that the thieves had entered from there.

"The Shrif had three people who were close to him, his brother, his uncle and his friend Mohammed. He had close relatives, of course, but he chose to go to his friend with this problem."

My grandmother knocked on the table and said, imitating first Mohammed and then Moulay Hfid, "'Who is it?' 'It's me.' 'What's the matter? Has something happened?' 'It's awful. Someone has taken my safe. It was full of gold. Five kilograms of gold...' his family jewelry. They were rich... 'and money and all my valuables.'"

My grandmother continued imitating the two men., " 'Who could do this? One man alone couldn't carry that safe.' 'And the people of your house, didn't they hear anything?' 'No, they didn't.'

"It was Mohammed's wife Zineb who related this to me. She's naive. She said that Mohammed said, 'Moulay Hfid! An outsider could not possibly have done this. It is one of your close friends, one of those who deal with you, someone who has shared food with you and been a guest in your house.'"

"How could he have the nerve to say this?" interjected my mother.

"'All their houses must be searched,' said Mohammed. 'An outsider could not have done this. Let's go to the police and have them search your friends' houses, including mine, so that it won't be said that you have excluded my house.' He thought they wouldn't move the iron and wood. He went with the Shrif to the police and they all went to the Shrif's house. They went up to the roof and saw where the thief might have entered. (I won't talk about that in detail.)

11

"They say that the police then started with Mohammed's house, because Mohammed himself insisted on it, even though the Shrif had said to him, 'I swear I will not search your house.' Mohammed had replied, 'I swear that it must be the first on the list, so that people will say you started with my house.'

"They entered Mohammed's house and searched all the rooms. Well, they did not shake things; a safe is not a needle. They looked in the garage and found nothing.

"Then a policeman saw the staircase to the cellar and suggested, 'Let's go down there.' Mohammed said, 'Okay!' They went and looked around and one of the policemen said, 'Let's pull down that iron and wood.'

"At that point the Shrif protested, 'What do you mean? It has been there for years and it is up to the ceiling.'

"The police said, 'We're going to pull it down anyway.' They pulled one post, then another and the pile of iron and wood collapsed..."

"It was loose. He did not pack it tight," my mother said.

"...and the safe appeared.

"The Shrif exclaimed, 'What!?'"

My grandmother raised her head in an attitude of shock. She bit her lip and closed her eyes in disgust, then went on: "Mohammed told them, 'Beating me is unnecessary. I'll explain everything to you.' They took him to the Shrif's house and he showed them how he managed the operation."

"And what was the sentence?" I asked.

"I'll get to that. The police kept Mohammed in Sefrou overnight and in the morning they took him to Fez. Then Zineb said that the house was too big, that she was afraid to be alone there. The house is by the river, under the bridge. She kept saying she was afraid to be there by herself, that she wanted to go to her father's house. So she went, and her husband was kept in Fez for three months before the sentence was pronounced.

"Some of those people who interfere in other people's business came to Zineb's father and told him, 'You are a good man, and our mayor, al-Bakkay, is a good man.' The father knew the mayor because the mayor sent his grain to be ground in his mill. 'Let your daughter give you some money, and you take it to Al-Bakkay. Maybe he'll reduce the sentence. If Zineb were here, I'd tell her that her poor father was a good man. He would never have had any experience with prison if her husband had not gotten into trouble. And then she'd start telling everything to everyone. She's so naive.'

"So Zineb's father went to al-Bakkay, kissed his shoulder and pleaded, 'Take this money, sir, and reduce my son-in-law's sentence.'

" 'What?' the mayor exclaimed. 'Do you think I would take bribery to overlook this robbery, this offense against religion? Lock him up!' And they locked him up too.

" They had been dealing with one prisoner and now they were dealing with two. I call on God.

"They condemned the father to three months in jail in Sefrou, and his poor daughter stayed in her father's house, enduring the long years until her husband got out of prison. And as I already told you, when, just recently, he did finally get out, he said he couldn't face the Shrif and other people, and he went to his father-in-law — who by now had served his sentence long before — and said to him, 'God has written in my destiny what has taken place. I have now decided to leave the town. I don't know what's in store for me and I don't want to drag your daughter to other people's hometowns. So if you want me to divorce her, I will.'

"And that's when the father-in-law said that he was a Muslim who bears witness that there is no God but God and that Mohammed is His Messenger, that he was neither a Jew nor a Christian and that he would never tell him to divorce her. Then he told him to take his wife and let her share his fate."

Then my grandmother concluded her story this way, "He will die without ever seeing his hometown again."

We all wiped our tears. Seized by the power and beauty of the narration, I said, "That's the sort of story I like, about real people, not like that story about the snake that came out of the drain and became a handsome young man, or that story about the bride who had her husband's wives stick needles in her head and turn her into a dove. Grandma! Tell us the story that asks, 'Can he who is in love sleep?' Tell it!"

Thirty-five years have now passed since Mohammed left his hometown and went to live in Rabat. As I was writing his story, I wondered about my grandmother's assertion that he would never again see his hometown. A relative of his, a friend of my mother's, happened to be visiting us at the time and I asked her, "So, does he ever go to his hometown?"

"He does," she said, "but he enters after sunset and leaves before dawn. He is never seen there during the day."

In El Ksiba, my father often used to stay away from home with his friends for an entire twenty-four hours, or even for several days at a time. In their absence, these men allowed their wives to invite each other to their homes, where they spent their time eating, drinking tea, beat-

13

ing drums, laughing, singing, ululating, talking loudly, and making allusions, with feigned indifference, to what their husbands might be doing. My mother laughed with them, but when we misbehaved she said, "May God bring down loss on your father and on him who matched me with him!"

The Moroccan elite, in that area at least, were enjoying themselves, allowing their wives to do likewise. After Independence, however, they would say, "That was a colonialist policy to distract people." "Colonialism instituted promiscuity and vulgarized wine."

The ladies' receptions involved much preparation. Furniture was taken out of the rooms. The house was washed. The silver trays were polished. On the day of the reception, the table was moved against the courtyard wall, and a plastic tablecloth was folded and left resting on the tabletop, to be spread when the table was put before the guests. The silver wash basin was set beside the table, with the kettle full of water and a folded towel so the guests could wash their hands before eating. Next to the washing things were all the tea sets with their sheer embroidered covers.

Whenever my grandmother was visiting during one of these receptions, she would sit on a floor cushion in the courtyard, cutting mint by the water fountain. My mother was in the room she used as a kitchen, her sleeves rolled up and her skirt tucked up under her checked apron. With a large wooden ladle in her hands, she stood among brass pots and braziers.

All the guests used to arrive together. There was Lalla Khaddouj from Boujad. She was the second wife of Ben Jilali of Fez, the scribe of the *caid* (local official) of El Ksiba. There was Titima, daughter of the caid and daughter-in-law of Ben Jilali, and Titima's mother Lalla Fettouma Cherkaouia. Cherkaouia also came from Boujad. She had been divorced by the caid and then married a prominent tradesman in the village.

In a cloud of perfumes, pulling down their face veils, the women would come in, sailing into the best room in a Moroccan house, the one reserved for guests, who usually were men. My mother would be proclaiming, "This is a great day!" and insisting that they take off their djellabas. They finally did, uncovering fine outfits that had been concealed by the outer garments: caftans, Fassi belts and slippers made with pure gold thread, emerald earrings dangling from their earlobes like suspended tears, gold bracelets from Essouira, necklaces of gold coins mixed with black beads.

The women sat down, wiped their faces with their embroidered handkerchiefs and adjusted their decorated scarves. My aunt Hachmia passed around the hand-washing utensils and towel, and they washed their hands. Then she brought in the table and put it in place. The food for me and my sisters was set on a separate table in the courtyard, but Fatiha usually started crying because she wanted to eat with the guests.

"What does she want?" Lalla Fattouma Cherkaouia asked my mother.

"Well, ma'am, she wants to eat with the guests. *She* thinks she is the caid's daughter."

"Bring her, for the love of God. Why don't you do something about that child, pass her under a camel for example? This hysterical behavior of hers is really too much."

My mother took Fatiha, and I stayed with Khadija in the courtyard, eating lemon chicken and dipping bread in its delicious sauce.

The guests feasted on lemon chicken, steamed lamb, grilled pepper and tomato salad, eggplant salad and lettuce tossed in sugar and orange-blossom water, and round slices of orange sprinkled with sugar, cinnamon and orange-blossom water.

Eating went on for hours. The women talked and laughed loudly as they ate, and my mother, who was proud of her city cooking, said every now and then, "Please eat! For the love of God. This is your house."

Finally the table was removed and my grandmother, who had been in the kitchen, and Khadija and I joined the guests. They spread out to be more comfortable and the tea set was put in front of Lalla Khaddouj, who was accorded the honor of conducting the tea-making ritual. Talking continued.

Lalla Fatouma Chekaouia often asked my mother, "Have you heard of your husband Si Hmed's latest affair?"

"Yes, yes. It's okay," said my mother, defiantly.

"She says it's okay," said Lalla Khaddouj, laughing.

My grandmother intervened, "Men are like that. My daughter can't complain, can she? She lacks nothing. We are often with her. How could she complain? Besides, all men are like that. No woman marries her father or brother."

Lalla Fettouma Cherkaouia changed the subject after my grandmother spoke up for my mother. "Where are the drums?" she asked. My mother brought them and they started the drumming and the ululating. Titima danced when her mother sang a song that was a hit at the time:

> Hey ma'am! What a sharp guy, hey ma'am!
> He sold the cheap and he bought the dear.
> He sold a *dfina* and bought a sewing
> machine, hey ma'am!
> Hey ma'am! The train came in, hey ma'am!
> Hey ma'am! We got in it and left, hey ma'am!

Hey ma'am! It took us to Essaouira, hey ma'am!
Hey ma'am! Do you know what we had for
lunch?
Hey Ma'am!

Hey ma'am! We had a kilo of tomatoes, hey
ma'am!
Hey ma'am! They were red and soft, hey
ma'am!
Hey ma'am! Do you know what we had for dinner? Hey ma'am!
Hey ma'am! We had a kilo of potatoes, hey
ma'am!
Hey ma'am! All white and shiny, hey ma'am!

Then my mother, whose sleeves were still rolled up, sang a city
song, beating her tambourine as she sang:

O girl, you torture me.
O girl, you torture me. You torment me with
those eyes of yours.
I pray to God to give me a little girl and I'll call
her Lalla Faouzia.
Then my heart will rest and be full of joy.
And I will give you all a party, my friends.

My mother always sang that song, and she always used the same
name, "Faouzia." It was the name of her baby, the little girl from her
first marriage whom she left with her mother when she moved with
my father to Moulay Ali Shrif, and who died of measles in her absence.
In the company of these women she seemed happy singing it, but when
she was alone I would see her crying quite often and hear her saying,
"O my mother! Here I am an outsider in other people's hometowns!"

Near the end of one of my grandmother's visits, she started talking
about leaving El Ksiba, but my mother wanted to delay the departure,
as she did with all of her relatives who came to visit. My grandmother
reminded her gently, "We have been here a month, daughter."

"Stay tomorrow, just tomorrow," pleaded my mother, and each
morning they repeated the same scene until my grandmother became
angry and said firmly, "Listen, I'm fed up with your tomorrows. Every
day you say "just tomorrow." I have my home too, you know, and my

16

place is there, and I swear that tomorrow I will not stay one more minute. Is that clear?"

My mother started to help my grandmother pack her family's bags. She stuffed things in and cried. The next morning they left carrying all their luggage. I went with them to the bus stop in front of the post office, but when they got there the guard told my grandfather, "You missed the bus. It went by half an hour ago." So they came back to our house. The next morning they left again, went to the bus stop and the guard told them the same thing.

"Strange!" my grandfather exclaimed.

"You come late," said the guard "and you say 'strange'?"

"Why? What time is it?"

"Six-thirty. The bus leaves at six. You come at six-thirty and say strange?"

"But it was five minutes to six when we left home. Strange indeed!"

When they returned to our house, they found out that my mother had been setting the clock back.

I hardly ever saw my father when we lived in El Ksiba. He was either with his friends somewhere else, or having his meals with them in the men's visiting room. He never ate with us, and my mother used to say critically, "He does not know how to eat without guests."

I froze with fear whenever I heard his cough from a distance. And whenever my mother said to me, "Wait till I get you," and wiped her mouth with her hand in a threatening gesture, adding "I swear by God I'll tell your father," I stopped at once whatever I was doing. He only spanked me twice. The first time, he did it because he saw me through the curtain of the doorway of the men's room. I was dancing to music on the radio. The second time it was because I went with some girls to peek into the contrôleur général's house where there was a dance party. I knew I should not have done this, but I wanted to see what a French party looked like. He spanked us hard on our bottoms the way the French did. It did not leave any lasting mark, but it burned and I remember it still.

Then we went to Sefrou — on that trip during which my father was arrested — and after that, I hardly saw him at all. When my mother told the story of his arrest, she always started with, "One day..."

"One day your father was at home and the office guard came and told him, 'The village tradesmen are at the office to complain about your friend Si Mouloud whom they want to send to jail.'"

"Why?" I interjected.

17

"Because the Nasara had exiled Si Mouloud from El Ksiba on account of his nationalistic activities. Later, they decided that exile was not enough, and they set the tradesmen against Si Mouloud. One of the Nasara told all the merchants, 'If you say he owes you money I will make you rich.'

"So your father went to the tradesmen and said, 'Okay, write down what he owes you on a piece of paper and give the paper to me.'

"My sisters and I had sold land we had inherited from my father," my mother went on, "and your father said to me, 'Go to Sefrou and send me your part of the money from the sale of that land. Send it in an express money order to pay the so-called debt of Si Mouloud, and if nothing happens to me I'll join you in Sefrou after eight days.'

" I said, 'All right.' I went to Sefrou and sent him the money and then the postman brought me a note asking me to come to the post office at a special time because Si Hmed Bouzid from El Ksiba was going to call me. Very few people had a telephone at home in those days. Bouazza went with me. The call came and he picked up the phone and he heard the words, 'I won't be able to come. Bring your sister at once.' Then I heard Bouazza say, 'You are not coming?' and I took the phone from him and said, 'But you said that you'd come,' and the voice at the other end of the line said, 'They did not give me a vacation.' And I said, 'You are not Si Hmed. That is not his voice.'

"We went home and I told my mother that the person on the phone said we must go to El Ksiba today. So we went, and Sidi Mohammed came with us. We stopped in Khenifra to change buses and when we got there we were told that our bus was leaving at dawn. A driver's assistant we knew took us to his home, and the next morning we took the bus and got off at the El Ksiba road sign. A truck came and Sidi Mohammed stopped it and the driver told him, 'I only have one place.'

"Sidi Mohammed said, 'It'll be only me. I'm going to tell my brother-in-law that his family is here so that he can pick them up.' He got in beside the driver and left, but we waited.

"Then there came the bus with Belaid, the driver's assistant, on its way from Beni Mellal. 'Oh lord!' he exclaimed when he heard that Sidi Mohammed had gone ahead to El Ksiba, 'Why did you send him there? Your house is guarded and nobody will dare to talk to him. People are scared, you know. Wait here for me. I'll take the mail to El Ksiba and be back. I'll take you to my house in Zaouit Cheikh to spend the night.'

"So, we went to Zaouit Cheikh. Am I clear? And when we got there Belaid's old mother started weeping and said, 'Oh, Lalla, two years is a long time.'

"I asked, 'Have they sentenced him already?'

"She replied, 'The Nasara sentenced him, and then sent him with a guard from one place to another. They tied a rope around him and tied it to the guard's horse and one guard passed him to another until they got to Rabat. They made him walk all the way.'

Belaid came in and I told him, 'Please, Belaid, for the love of God, there were passengers from Beni Mellal on the bus. They'll tell my in-laws that they saw us and there will be chaos and nobody will know where we are. Please help us go to Beni Mellal.'

"Well, he did. He took us out to the road and stopped a bus and told the driver, 'These are Si Hmed's wife and daughters,' and some men gave us their seats and sat on the floor. We got to your paternal grandfather's house and found it crowded. Said, your paternal uncle, and his cousin Robio had already gone to the El Ksiba sign and started calling for me, 'Fettouma! Fettouma!' When they could not find us they said, 'Perhaps they went to El Ksiba.'

"They went there and found Sidi Mohammed crying in the street by our house. Night had fallen. The guard assigned to watch our house had told him, 'Stay here, but if you see any Nasara, go away, and if no one comes you can stay and we'll see what will happen about your situation.' Whenever Sidi Mohammed saw friends of your father's he tried to talk to them, but they'd look frightened and turn away and continue walking.

"So we got to Beni Mellal and lamented with the others. Then we heard that a local man had seen your father somewhere in Rabat, with a guard. The man had kept looking at him and the guard said, 'You can talk to him if you like. There is no Nasrani* around.'

"That man brought the news that your father had told him: 'They took me to Oued-Zem, then to Khouribga and then to Berrachid. I was kept there overnight and then sent on my way the next morning with another guard, and now they have brought me to Rabat.' Said heard that news, brought it home and burst into tears as he relayed it.

"Your poor grandmother Khadija started beating her breast, and when the crying stopped I told your grandfather, 'Well, Sidi, now that we know where he is, let's go to see him—Said, Ma'ti and myself.'

"And he answered, 'No, ma'am. He's my son, but he left me nothing when he decided to go to prison. Why should I visit him? He doesn't care about his duty to me. And what harm have the Nasara done to us anyway? It is in their time that we came to have running water and electricity and clean streets. I will not visit him. Let them kill him if they want to.'

"I said, 'If that's the way you feel, then I will not stay here.'

---

* Singular of the plural Nasara

19

"'Fine. Good-bye,' he said. Your grandfather's first wife, or maybe someone else, said, referring to me, 'She has not stopped crying since she arrived.' And some other woman said, 'She should cry, shouldn't she?' And the first woman said, 'She's crying because Said and Ma'ti are wearing her husband's shirts and shoes and we are using her kitchenware and her pillows and mattresses.'

"I protested, 'That's not what worries me now. It's just the idea of jail. I never had anything to do with jail in my life.'

"And your grandfather retorted, 'I say we are not going to visit him.' And I said, 'I don't have the money to buy a bus ticket.' And he said, 'Too bad.'

"'Well,' I said, 'give me my car and Lalla Mahjouba's son will drive me. It's our car after all, isn't it? We bought it, my mother, my brother Bouazza and I.'

"He said, 'What car? There is no car anymore. I don't know where it is.'

"Lalla Mahjouba's son came in with Said and they said to me, 'We'll drive you as far as Azrou but you'll have to continue on your own.' I agreed.

"So, Bouazza, your sisters, you and I, we all went to Azrou and spent the night there at my sister Khnata's house. In the morning, Said and Lalla Mahjouba's son ate breakfast and left, and Khnata took us to the bus station. It was a Wednesday; I still remember. We took the bus and got to Sefrou in the evening. My uncle came to see me and started crying and everything, then he asked, 'What are your plans?'

" I said, 'Tomorrow is Thursday, Sidi, and Friday we'll go to visit him.' And he said, 'Do you know Rabat? Of course you don't.' I said, 'I'll ask.' (So anyway, I'll be brief.) 'And do you have money?' he asked, and I said, 'I'll borrow it and when I come back I'll sell something.' He said 'Well, my dear, I cannot help you.' 'We don't expect you to help, Sidi,' I replied.

"Your grandmother said, 'No one can help except God.' But then she added, 'I have your sisters' rent. Let's use it. Who's going with you?'

" I replied, 'You, Mother, and Bouazza.' Your grandmother still had some strength."

"So we got to Rabat and did not know where to go. We asked for directions and found our way to the jail. I asked some people there how we could visit a prisoner and they said, 'Is this your first visit?' 'Yes.' 'Your prisoner might not be allowed to have visitors,' they said, 'but you can buy him some food, if you like.' It was Friday and the Muslim shops were closed. In those days they used to close on Fridays. So I went and bought cigarettes and bread and jam and all that was necessary from a Jew. Then I came back to the jail. I took my apron and tied everything in it. I knew that he would recognize the apron. Then we put the bundle in the line with other people's food.

"Well, the guard came and began to take the food inside and a Nasrani guard called me and asked, 'How is the prisoner related to you?' 'He's my husband,' I said. 'Where do you live?' 'In Sefrou.' He took my bundle inside and then a Moroccan guard came out and asked, 'Why was this man put in jail? Is it for nationalism?' 'Yes,' I answered. 'What's his name?' 'Ahmed Bouzid.' 'I'm going to talk to him before that infidel comes back and see if he knows whether he can have visitors, so that you won't have to wait.'

"When he returned, he explained, 'Your husband has counter-sued the Nasara because they went into his house and searched it in his absence, and for that reason he can't have any visitors. You can go to the administration, your husband says, and ask for Mr. So-and-so, and when you find him, tell him you're Bouzid's wife and see if he will give you permission to visit. Tell him to write down the names of the people who are with you so that no one will be left out.'

"'Okay,' I said to him, and then I told Grandma: 'Stay here with the girls. I'll be back.'

"So I went with Bouazza to the administration building in the Touarga neighborhood. Taxis did not exist then. There were only carriages pulled by horses. We had to walk all the way. When we got there we found a man locking the doors. We said, 'Please, sir.' And the man said, 'Well ma'am, they have all left. What's the matter?' We told him and he said, 'Go to Moulay Driss...' I'm sorry, I mean Moulay Al Hassan Mausoleum '...and stay there. When the sultan's procession to the mosque for the Friday prayer is over, come back. Be here at two and I'll let you in first.'

"So we went. Bouazza started to cry, and I asked, 'What's the matter?' 'I have no money to buy cigarettes,' he said. I knew that he smoked, although he never did it in front of me. I would often find the smell of it in the toilet, but I had always pretended I didn't know. That day, I gave him enough money to buy two or three cigarettes. We stayed in that mausoleum with people telling their stories to each other. (Don't be impatient. I won't take any more time on this part. I'll soon get to the part about what happened at the jail.) When the sultan finished his Friday prayer and people started leaving the mosque I said to Bouazza, 'Let's go.'

"We went back to the door man at the administration building and he told everybody in the waiting room, 'This woman was here before,' and they said, 'Let her in first.' He said, 'Have a seat.'

21

"When the official came I went in, and he asked, 'How is the prisoner related to you?' 'He is my husband.' 'He is in real trouble,' he told me. 'He worked for the Nasara and he read the papers that had been put in the wastebasket and passed information on to the nationalists. But I'll give you the permits to visit him and we'll leave the rest to God. How many people are with you?' 'Myself, my mother, my brother and my young daughters—there are three of them.' He said, 'I'll give you passes for six persons.'

"I took the passes and we went back to the prison and I gave them to the Nasrani guard at the gate. He went inside, then came back and said, 'He is not allowed to have visitors, because he sued the contrôleur général.'

"So we had no choice. We returned to Sefrou and stayed there anxiously waiting while months passed. I went back and forth between Sefrou and Rabat every now and then, taking food to the prison, and every time they returned the empty pots to me I knew that he realized I had come.

"One day we got to the jail and found a Moroccan police officer from Beni Mellal. He asked, 'So, you are waiting around this place?' 'Yes.' I said. He said, 'That husband of yours is a bastard, a worthless bastard. He is not allowed to have visitors, but I'll arrange for you to visit him so that he will know what influence I have.' I said nothing. He pressed the bell and a Moroccan guard opened the door and said, 'Stay where you are. It is not time for visitors yet.' The police officer took out his badge and the guard saluted him and opened the door. He entered and I followed him.

" The police officer called another Moroccan guard and said, 'Bring Ahmed Bouzid,' and the guard went in and brought your father behind the wire screen. The police officer said to him sarcastically, 'How are you enjoying this?' Your father replied defiantly, 'It's great!' The police officer ignored this and continued: 'I mean, why are you against the Nasara? What have they done to you?' 'That's my business and if one is going to die, it's better to die for a good cause. But why are you talking to me? What do you want?' 'What do I want? I want to have a couple of words with you, then I want to have a guard bring you outside the screen so you can see what influence I have.'

"So a guard led the police officer and me to a courtyard and they brought your father there. The police officer said to him, 'She's living in Sefrou now,' (meaning me) '...Tell her to stop coming all that way with food. I'll be staying in Rabat for a while and I will send you *harira* soup and some food.' It was Ramadan. Your father said, 'I will never eat your harira. My wife will bring me food and if she does not there is the jail food. Okay?' 'Are you saying you don't deign to eat my food?' 'Yes,' said your father. 'That's exactly what I am saying.'

"So, anyway, we went home again. Eventually they started allowing us to visit him regularly. Once we found your father's half-brother Mohammed, waiting at the prison gate and he asked, 'How are you?' I said, 'Okay.' He said, 'They say I need a permit. I don't know where to go for one.' And your grandma said, 'Give him my permit, daughter.' And I did.

"We entered and Mohammad asked your father, 'May Fettouma go with me to Beni Mellal?' 'It's up to her now. She may, of course, but listen,' your father said, turning to me: 'The house you own in Sefrou... Some people want to rent it and want to get in touch with you.' (He meant the nationalists. I didn't own any house. The nationalists wanted to send me money and your father was using this way of telling me because he knew that the guard wouldn't understand.) I said, 'Okay,' and he said, 'Go with Mohammed now.' So I went. Oh, I forgot, your father had said before, 'Wait outside, I'll write a letter for you to take to my father, but first I must give it to the prison director for his approval.' So we went out and waited until a guard came and asked, 'Who is here to visit Ahmed Bouzid?' 'I am.' 'Here's a letter from him.' I took it and we left.

"So we went to your grandfather's house in Beni Mellal. It's useless to talk of the problem I had with Kabboura in Beni Mellal. It would take too long. She and her husband had been in Casablanca to attend a celebration of the birth of a son of that same Moroccan police officer who called your father a bastard and who collaborated with the Nasara. Mohammed told everybody about that as soon as we arrived at the house. Your poor grandmother was upset by that and started slapping her cheeks with both hands, saying, 'He who does not visit my son in prison is not my friend,' meaning Kabboura and her husband who did the long trip to attend that traitor's celebration instead of visiting your father in the prison.

"Then your cousin Aicha went to her aunt Kabboura and told her, 'That woman of Sefrou, Si Hmed's wife, has said that you will never be her friend because you went to that police officer's celebration instead of visiting her husband in prison.' But I never said that, I swear. I have no reason to lie now after all these years.

"In the evening Kabboura came with her mother. They were angry because of Aicha's story. The house was crowded and I had Naima on my lap, and Kabboura's mother started making threatening motions and saying to me, 'Is that so, woman of Sefrou? That I will never be your friend? Do you know why they have arrested your lord and master? Because of his relations with other women.'

"I turned to your grandfather and said, 'What do you think of this, Sidi? The house is full of people and they are insulting me and nobody stands up for me.' He replied, 'Well, they're guests in my house. I can say nothing to them.'

"I then turned to Kabboura and said, 'If my husband had other women, it was your husband who played the lute for him in those wicked parties of theirs, and I hear his singing was like the howls of a dog. Yes, my husband drank wine, but yours drank the dregs from his glass.'

"She said, 'You runt of a rat!' and I said, 'You're nothing but a piece of river cane, and the current will uproot you and carry you away!'

"So anyway, that same day I said to your grandfather, 'Here, Sidi this letter is from your son.' He could not read, of course, so he took it and called to his son, 'Ma'ti! Ma'ti! Come and see what's in this letter!'

"Ma'ti's wife took it to her husband in his room to read it there and we waited and waited and waited until he came out and your grandfather finally said, 'Well?'

"Ma'ti said, 'This letter was not written by my brother. Her brother Bouazza wrote it. That's not Si Hmed's handwriting.'

" I told the father, 'This son of yours Ma'ti is not educated enough to read any letters. Can't he see the prison stamp and the director's signature and everything?'

"But that old man shook his head and argued with me. 'Ma'ti,' he said, 'has no reason to lie.'

"I said, 'Well then, take it to the person who used to read the letters that your son sent you when he lived in Moulay Ali Shrif. He would know if it's from Si Hmed.' Your grandfather insisted, 'I say it is not my son's letter. Bring it here.' And he took it and went out .

"Bouazza told me, 'Come inside, sister.' (We were in the courtyard.) 'They might harm you. Let's lock the door from inside while we wait for them to decide about the letter.'

"'Okay,' I said. So we went in one of the rooms and locked the door.

"Then into the courtyard came Zahra, your father's half-sister, and we could hear them telling her what had been said. She came to the window and started shouting to me through the ironwork, 'You so-and-so! Who do you think you are? You and your family have taken advantage of my brother's money. Take this!' She rudely gestured with her middle finger through the ironwork, and I caught that finger of hers and I pressed it hard against a bar. I kept pushing and pushing while she screamed and screamed, and then we heard a knock on the door. Bouazza opened it and I let go of rude Zahra's finger.

24

It was your father's cousin Robio at the door, may God bless his soul. Unlike your father's other relatives, he stood by me like a man. He came in and said, 'Don't be scared.'

" I said, 'God is above us all.'

"He said, 'Uncle Hammadi is going to sue you and has gone to the court house. He is charging you with forgery.'

"I asked, 'What am I to do? And what about the girls? I can't leave them here.'

"He said, 'Don't worry about the girls. Bouazza will carry Fatiha, I'll carry Naima, and Leila will walk, and I'll go with you to the courthouse.'

"So we went to the courthouse and found your grandfather sitting outside the courtroom. A guard came out and called his name and mine. We entered and stood in front of the *cadi*, the judge. He said nothing to your grandfather, but he — I mean the cadi — said to me, 'Why were you away when your husband was arrested?'

"Your grandfather quickly said, 'He had divorced her.' The cadi told him to shut up, and I told the cadi what I have just told you, that I went to Sefrou to get my part of the money from the sale of the land my sisters and I had inherited from my father and that I sent it to my husband in an express money order so that he could pay his friend's so-called debt.

"The cadi said, 'Do you have the receipt to show me?' (I swear, daughter, by all that I have done for you, that it was right there in my purse in my pocket.) I said, 'Oh yes, I do. Here it is.'

"And he said, 'Give it to me.' He read it and said to your grandfather, 'What can I say? You are a mean and unjust person. How dare you say your son divorced her? The receipt says that she is sending the money to Ahmed Bouzid in El Ksiba. Your son is struggling for the country and for his countrymen. Is this *your* struggle? How dare you seize her furniture?' (I had told him that they had taken it.) He repeated, 'How could you take her furniture?'

"Your grandfather said, 'My son supported us and now he is in prison for his nationalist activities. I'm old and I have to start selling his furniture to support us. She doesn't own a nail in it. Everything belongs to my son.'

"The cadi asked, 'Is that the truth?'

" 'Yes,' he answered.

"And the cadi said, 'Well then, where is the so-called forged letter?'

"Your grandfather handed it to him and the cadi read it and said scornfully, 'There are no words in which I can express the meanness of your behavior. The letter says, "Dear Mother and Father, I ask you, by all that you have done for me and by all that I have done for you, to treat this woman well. Give her the car and her furniture and let her go in peace to her hometown.'"

"'That letter is forged, sir,' insisted your grandfather. '...and that's the one who wrote it.'

"He pointed to Bouazza, who said, 'If it can be proved that I wrote that letter, then put me in jail too, sir, and I'll get through it or else perish.'

"The cadi said, 'Listen, this is going on too long. It's one o'clock. Go now and come back at two.'

"Your grandfather said, 'I forbid this woman to set foot in my house.'

"But Robio said, 'She's welcome in mine, sir.'

"And the cadi asked him, 'How is she related to you?'

"He replied, 'She isn't, sir. It's he who is related to me. He is my maternal uncle. She is only my uncle's daughter-in-law. She has always been very nice to us.'

"The cadi said, 'May God reward you, son. I swear, if that man in prison had not been struggling for our nation, I'd have had to send his wife with the other beggars until this is settled.'

"Robio said, 'She's welcome in my house. And sir, everything she told you is true. I was visiting when the express money order arrived, and I saw the money.'

"We went to Robio's house and were greeted by his mother, bless her soul, and his wife, may God bless her soul too if she's dead, or mention her with good words if she's still alive. We had a gloomy lunch, left the girls there and went back to the courthouse. We found him—I mean the old man—firmly seated on a chair outside the courtroom.

"They called us and the cadi talked to your grandfather about something different. He asked, 'And now what are you going to do about the furniture and all that?' 'We won't give her a single needle. Everything belongs to my son.' 'Oh does it?' 'Yes.' 'Did your son give you a permit to take it?' 'Mm... he did not, but he supported us and I took his furniture to sell it.' 'Listen, tomorrow at dawn I want an official designated by the court to go with this lady, her brother, and your son Ma'ti, the one who sold the car...' (Oh, I forgot, before that, the cadi asked your grandfather, 'Where is your son? the one who sold the car?' 'He is out of town.' The cadi said, 'He'll have to return, sooner or later.')

"So anyway the cadi said, 'Tomorrow the four people I mentioned will have to be at the bus station. I have decided that you must go to Rabat to see this woman's husband at the prison, so you can hear what he has to say and this dispute can be settled. You, sir,' he said to your grandfather, 'you must cover all their expenses.'

"Earlier, I had told the cadi that whenever I went to Rabat to see your father I had no place to stay. My sister Zhor lived there, but her husband was working for the Nasara and he was afraid he would lose his job if I stayed in their house. His mother had come to Grandma in Sefrou and told her, 'He's worried. He says that now they have brought Si Hmed to prison in Rabat, relatives will be coming from Sefrou and Beni Mellal and he fears that his connection with them could cost him his job.'

"The cadi continued: 'You'll all go to a hotel. The official assigned by the court and Ma'ti will stay in one room and this woman will stay in another room with her brother. Remember, Hammadi Bouzid, you will pay the expenses. The official will go to the prison with them and find out whether that letter was forged or not. That's all I have to say now.'

"We went to Robio's house and he went out to look for Ma'ti and found out that he had gone to Rabat to visit his brother in prison where he would probably be giving him a false version of what had happened. Robio, poor man, came back and said, 'The son of a bitch is trying to see Si Hmed before us.'

"But we heard later that through God's omnipotence the guards did not allow him to enter the prison. So anyway, Robio's mother told me, 'Leave the girls with me and go, and if your husband says that it's not his letter don't come back. Don't make yourself and us look ridiculous. But if he says that it *is* his letter and stands up for you, then do come back. You'll be welcome.'

"And I said, 'Look, Lalla Fettouma, I won't leave the girls here, because if things turn against me I won't come back.' While we continued discussing what to do, Robio went to the blind man who was supervising the intercity bus company at that time, and he gave Robio two free tickets. Even though it was late, Robio's wife made bread for us to take on the trip. So, Bouazza and I left on the bus. (Don't worry, I won't take much longer to finish this story.) We got to Rabat and went to the administrative office and I asked for permits for three: one for me, one for the court official, and one for my brother Bouazza. They gave them to me and we went to the prison.

"When we arrived there a lorry loaded with inmates came and started backing up to the gate. As I moved out of its way I saw the court official sitting on a low wall with Ma'ti, and I looked away. They started letting visitors in. I had not brought any food.

"The guard said, 'Don't you have any food?'

" I said, 'No, sir.' I gave him the permits and the official and Ma'ti stood behind me.

"The guard asked them, 'Where are your permits?' And the official said, 'We're with this woman. We've been sent here by the court.'

"We entered and Si Hmed came and asked, 'How are you? How are the girls?' and so on, and then he asked me, 'What did you do about the house?' 'What house?' I said and I told him what had happened in Beni Mellal.

"He asked Ma'ti, 'What's your version?' 'It is as she says,' he replied.

"Then Si Hmed looked at the official and asked, 'Why is this man with you?' and the official said, 'I'm sent by the court, sir, to find out if you wrote a letter to your father telling him to give your wife your car and her belongings.'

" 'Yes I did,' said Si Hmed. 'Didn't the cadi see the prison stamp and the signature of the director?' The official said, 'You want her to have everything?' Si Hmed replied, 'If she says that a nail in the wall is hers, then it is. I don't own a needle of that dowry. Everything belongs to her. And this one' (he pointed to Ma'ti) 'ought to be punished for selling the car. How dare he sell my car when I am in prison?'

"The guard interrupted, 'Hey! This isn't a court.' 'Yes it is,' said Si Hmed. 'They've been sent here by a court.' The guard went out and brought the director, who told us to leave.

"So anyway, we left, and when we were outside Ma'ti made a circle with his thumb and forefinger, raised it in front of my face and said, 'You'll get your goods when you can pass through here.' 'We're still at the prison gate,' I retorted, and he said, 'If you can reach your husband now, chop off his head and hit me with it.' I pointed my forefinger to the sky and said, 'I leave retribution to Him.'

"I returned to Beni Mellal and went to Robio's house. Then a letter came from the cadi summoning us all to return to the courtroom.

" We stood in front of him and he asked my father-in-law, 'What do you say now?' 'I still say it is not my son's letter,' replied the old man. 'We have passed that stage of the case, sir. Now, two court officials will go to your house and Si Hmed's wife will take her belongings. I don't want any other woman there to cause any trouble. If a needle is missing you will replace it with a mattress needle.'

"Everybody went out of your grandfather's house, even your father's mother, who was sick and had to be carried. Robio went to a truck driver and told him, 'We need you at such and such a time to transport Si Hmed's furniture to Sefrou.' We went back to Robio's house and had another gloomy lunch. (I'll be brief and to the point.)

We went to your grandfather's house after the afternoon prayer. Some men, members of the nationalist movement came, and also the porters. One of the officials said to me, 'Take your time, Lalla, and make sure nothing is missing.' After I went in and looked around I told

Bouazza that a radio set and two large batteries were missing. He said, 'Don't introduce another problem, please. If you tell them that now they'll delay our departure and we should not stay at our hosts' house any longer.'

"So, the porters brought everything and loaded it all in the truck. The driver told Robio and Bouazza, 'I'm going to drive at night. If the road police stop us and ask me how I am related to her, I'll say that I'm her husband and that we were living in Beni Mellal, but now I'm out of work and we are going to her hometown. If we are not stopped, so much the better.' I didn't want to ask how much he had charged. The nationalists who were standing there had paid him.

"We all got to Sefrou with the first daylight. Nobody stopped us on the way. There was nobody on that road except God. We got to Bab al Maqam in Sefrou and who should appear but Moulay Ali, poor man! May God bless his soul. He was the head of all the porters.

"He said, 'Hello! Welcome! Has anything happened to Si Hmed? Has he passed away? Have they killed him?'

"'No.' I said. 'It's only the Nasara. They said that the house in El Ksiba had to be emptied, that everything had to be moved away.' I was in no mood to relate the whole story.

"Moulay Ali called the porters and told them, 'Come, pack everything up and take it to the house of this lady's father.' Then he said to me, 'Go home now. I'll take care of everything and join you'.

"They moved everything and when Moulay Ali joined us I asked him, 'How much shall I pay them?' He gestured with his forefinger, putting it on his temple and wiggling it back and forth as if to say 'Are you crazy?' He said, 'They have done this job with pleasure and have prayed to God for Si Hmed. And you talk of paying them! Don't be silly. He is no common prisoner. He's a nationalist.'

"Your grandmother, bless her soul, had already prepared breakfast for Moulay Ali and the porters. Some bread, black olives, preserved served meat, and tea. They ate it and left."

29

Chapter II
SEFROU

I woke up that next morning and found porters putting banquettes on one side of the courtyard, lining up mattresses on them and then rushing out. Women were coming to visit. Every time a new group arrived they would cry and cry and my mother cried with them. She would wipe her eyes and start telling them the story again from the beginning: "One day..." The women listened in silence, clicked their tongues and sighed every now and then.

Two days later my aunt Khnata came. She hugged my mother saying, "My long suffering little sister!"

Then she sat down and announced, "Your suffering is wasted. Apparently your husband has a second wife. God and the blood you share with him have caught him. Driss and I were visiting Zhor and we went out for a walk and Driss said, 'Let's go past the prison and ask about the formalities of visits.' So we did, and while we were there a woman came and delivered a food basket in your husband's name, saying that she was his sister-in-law. Now if you are a true member of our family, don't go near that jail again."

They talked about that subject all evening.

Next morning my mother's old aunt Zineb came to the house, walking all bent over, her *haik* wrapped around her. She sat in the middle of Grandma's room on the ground floor and gave her opinion of the situation: "Well, you gave him the car and he gave it to his family. He is an outsider, and we used to say that didn't matter, but now he has secretly taken a second wife." She followed this with a variation of my aunt Khnata's advice: "Now if you are a true woman of Sefrou, and the daughter of your father, you should never set foot in that jail again."

My mother remained silent, but when her aunt left she said to my grandmother, "If you agree with what Khnata and my aunt say, don't come with me, because I am determined to continue to visit that jail, and when he gets out I'll ask him for my papers and what the law provides. If I don't go, people will say, 'She and her family have taken advantage of his money and now she has let him down.'"

"I'll go with you," answered my grandmother. "I don't care what they say."

And they left us, the children, with Sidi Mohamed's family. He was the son of my mother's old aunt Zineb. My mother and grandmother went to the prison, and when they got back, many women came to visit and mother told the story over and over again about what had happened during that visit to Rabat.

"We arrived on Friday. I put the food in line and joined the queue of visitors. A woman stood behind me. A guard came and asked the name of my detainee. I told him and he asked me, 'How is he related to you?' I said, 'He is my husband.' Then he told the woman behind me, 'How about you?' and she replied, 'I'm sorry sir, I'm waiting for my mother. I'll get out of the line if you want me to.' But when he left she said to me, 'I want to tell you something, Lalla. My husband cannot have visits and so I've been delivering his food in your husband's name, pretending that I was his sister-in-law.' (I'll tell you her name later.) '...May I enter with you?'

"I gave her my mother's permit and we entered. Si Hmed was brought in and she said to him, 'The Blue Angel visited me last night.' She reported what he had said, then asked: 'May I take your wife and her mother home with me?' He agreed and when we left the prison I asked her, 'Where do you live?' 'In Salé,' she said, 'across the river from Rabat.' And I said, 'First, I have to let the people I'm staying with know where I'm going. They live near the rug market. I'll leave my mother with you.'

"I found Si Abdelkader Ben Youssef at home (he was the man of the house where I was staying) and he asked, 'What's the news? Are there any new detainees?' He wanted to know, because he prepared food for all of them; he'd been told to do so by the nationalist movement. I told him about this woman and said that she had permission from Si Hmed to take me to her house in Salé. He asked, 'Did she talk to him? Did he see her?'

"When I said yes, he said, 'Go back to that woman. I have the list of all the detainees. Ask her what her name is and her husband's.' When I went back to her, she said, 'Tell him I'm Touria Sekkat and my husband is Mohammed Asafi.' Then I reported their names to Si Abdelkader, as he had told me to do.

"My mother and I went with Touria Sekkat to her home and in the evening a man came. He had long hair down to his shoulders and was wearing a torn djellabah and an old pair of sandals tied with rope. She took him to the guest room and my mother whispered, 'Daughter, that man's face is familiar. He looks like one of the prison guards. His nose has the same tattoo.' I found out later that he was the one called the Blue Angel, who passed on letters and information to the detainees.

And there was another story that my mother would begin with the words, "One day..." This was the story she told often until after Morocco got its independence, the story that went back to the day of my father's first arrest.

31

"One day the sultan told his Moroccan people to fast in protest against the French assassination of the Tunisian unionist Farhat Hachad. The news came to Si Hmed after the afternoon prayer. He went to Beni Mellal to tell his friends there, and when he came back the police stopped him at the El Ksiba road sign. They asked him where he had been and he replied, 'In Beni Mellal.' Then they asked him what he had been doing there. 'I heard that my father was sick and went to see him,' he replied. He reached El Ksiba and went straight to the *mouqaddam* (district officer) in the village. It was a Saturday evening and Sunday is the market day there. 'Tell the people about the sultan's decree,' your father said, 'and the reason for that decree. Tell everyone now so they won't eat tomorrow and so the doughnut sellers and the kebab stands won't prepare any food. Everybody in Morocco should fast tomorrow.' But the Nasara caught the mouqaddam spreading that information and when they asked him where he got it, he said, 'From Si Hmed Bouzid.'

"They did not arrest Si Hmed then, but by the time I went to Sefrou they had forbidden him to have any contact with anyone in the village. He was at home with Ben Jilali, whom he considered his best friend, when someone brought him some nationalist tracts. He took them and said to his friend, 'Look! Isn't this great? When will you decide to join us?' Then he put the tracts on his desk, shaved and changed his clothes, and they both left for work. He went to his office, but Ben Jilali went to the contrôleur général and said, 'I know the person who delivers the tracts in El Ksiba. It is Bouzid. His wife is in Sefrou. The tracts are on his desk at his house.' The Nasrani went to the house, took the tracts, called Si Hmed in, and personally put handcuffs on him and put him in a cell. He was left there for two days. Then the Nasrani summoned him and demanded, 'How can you work for us and do this?' He pointed at the tracts. Si Hmed said, 'My allegiance is to my country, not to yours.' The Nasrani stood up and slapped him on the face. Then Si Hmed kicked the Nasrani in the stomach so hard that he fell into a chair. 'Be a witness to this,' the Nasrani said to the caid whom he had called in to be present at the interview. But the caid said, 'You slapped him first. He's handcuffed and so he had to use his foot. Question him if you want to, but don't hit him.'

"The next day the Nasrani sentenced my Si Hmed to two years in prison and sent him to Rabat. Seven months later the Nasara judged him in Rabat, decided that he deserved a longer sentence for his offense, and said, 'The two years will start now.' Do you see what I mean?

"When the Nasrani in El Ksiba heard the news of the judgment, he asked that Si Hmed be sent back to him so that he could have the satisfaction of deciding how the sentence should be served. When he got back to El Ksiba, Si Hmed found they had arrested all his nationalist friends — Khallaf the butcher and the others. The Nasrani ordered them all to dig a well near the French resort in Taghbalout.

"Si Hmed's mother traveled from Beni Mellal to visit him in Taghbalout and brought food for him. She went to the French administration building. A guard named Brahim took her aside near a wall, started crying and said, 'You can't see him, Lalla. He's down in a deep well, where they have him digging. He's not allowed out of it.'

"She returned to Beni Mellal, threw the food away in the street, went home, started slapping her cheeks, then fell and lost consciousness. *Faqihs* (religious specialists) were fetched, to read the Qur'an by her bed all night, but before the sunset call to prayer she passed away.

"Thus, Si Hmed's poor mother returned to Beni Mellal and died, and he stayed in the well with his fellow detainees, digging and digging, filling a large vat with earth and rocks, which was pulled up by another detainee to be emptied out on the ground above them. But one day the vat hit the wall and a rock fell on one of the men who was digging. He cried out, 'God!' and fell down. The guard looked into the well and called out, 'What is it? Who screamed?' They said, 'A rock fell on...' (I cannot remember the name of the man.) 'We don't know how badly he's hurt. He can't speak.' The guard emptied the vat and sent it back down and told them to put the injured man in it, and he and the detainee at the top pulled it up. They laid him in the sun. The guard jumped on his horse and went to El Ksiba to inform the Nasrani, who mounted his horse and rode back with him to the well. But when he saw the man lying in the sun he said to the guard, 'You've dealt with the situation, haven't you? You got him out of the well. Why did you bother to call me?' He took off the guard's official robe, put handcuffs on him, and ordered someone to take him to jail. Then the Nasrani leaned over the well and called, 'Bouzid!' And your father replied, 'Yes?' 'Why don't you call the nationalists to save you? Don't you realize that you will perish down there?' And Si Hmed called back, 'Don't go. I have something to say to you. One dies only once, so one might as well die for a good cause. I dare you to bring a piece of marble and some concrete and seal me up in this well right now.'

"The nationalist prisoners finally finished digging the well. It's still there. They call it Ben Bouzid's well.

"After that, they took Si Hmed and his fellow detainees to the desert and forced them to carry sand from one place to another. At night, though, through the power of God, the sand would go back where it was before; it had been blown by the wind. When relatives visited the prisoners in the desert, they could only look at them from a distance. But the guards were human; when there was no Nasrani around they let the relatives talk with the prisoners. After six months the Nasrani of El Ksiba felt that his desire to punish Si Hmed had been satisfied and he sent him back to the prison in Rabat.

"Then one day, as winter came on, my sister Zhor was getting ready to celebrate the circumcision of her sons and I received a letter from Si Hmed. Zhor and her husband had come from Rabat to Sefrou to hold the circumcision ceremony. They were at the husband's parents' house. I could not read the letter and so I took it there and found Zhor giving instructions to her husband's aunt, who was on her way out to deliver the oral invitations to the circumcision. Some women were ululating in the courtyard, getting in a happy mood. I was a fool then, I think. I had no common sense. I said to Zhor's husband, 'Please, Omar, read this letter for me.' He took it and started shaking all over, then gave it back to me and said, 'Leave me alone.' He was afraid to come near anything related with the nationalists because he worked for the Nasara.

"I went back home to my father's house and my brother Bouazza came and read the letter. He told me what it said: Si Hmed was going to be transferred with eleven other detainees somewhere and they had no warm clothes. I was supposed to come immediately to the prison in Rabat with warm clothing ... and he gave a list.

"There was a Shrif who had a shop near the courthouse. I don't suppose you'd remember him. He sold shirts and wool vests. I took the letter to him, because he had once told me, 'If your husband ever needs any clothes, come and get them. I'll not sell them to you at a profit. You can pay me whenever you can.' I gave him the letter. He read it silently and started crying. Then he said, 'He says they're going to transfer them to another prison and that he needs vests, shirts, scarves and wool djellabahs.' He cried as he spoke, and I cried too. He stopped and said, 'Don't cry. You can't read the list of the clothes mentioned in this letter, but I can. Leave it with me. I'll gather together everything. Don't give me a franc now.' Oh, I forgot; the letter said, '...and send some dried meat, too.'

"Let's not talk about Zhor and how she celebrated when I was in such distress. Your grandmother said, 'If I go with you now, Zhor will say I left her. You go and leave your girls here with me.'

"So I went with Bouazza to Rabat where we stayed at Ben Youssef's. The next morning we took the food and clothes from the Shrif's shop to the prison. There we saw a truck loading detainees. Two long wooden planks lay up against the back of the truck. The detainees, who were handcuffed, were climbing awkwardly up the planks, while two Nasara stood in the bed of the truck, one on each side, grabbing the men and throwing them into the truck, where they fell on top of one another like watermelons. They couldn't do anything else, because they were handcuffed. Some relatives of the detainees stood nearby watching, and the men started to protest. 'How dare you treat them like that? Either let them climb up by themselves or else...' The Nasara argued, 'They'll fall.' But the protesters answered, 'Let them fall. It's better than treating them like watermelons. If you throw one more we'll make trouble.' The protesters kept shouting at the Nasara, and the women cried and cried.

"The detainees coming out of the prison said to us, 'Look what's going on. Don't try to visit us now. When we get settled wherever they're taking us, we'll write.'

"All the men were taken to al-'Ader prison, south of Casablanca, and I started visiting your father there. That's why my hearing has gotten so bad, I think. I had to keep my djellabah hood on my head for days at a time, and even though this made me sweat I couldn't take it off until I got home. In those days I wore a face veil, too, and had to cover my head, so when I came back sweating I'd take off the hood and the veil and catch cold.

"One day a man came to the prison and put a food basket in the line, and when the French guard asked him, 'What's your prisoner's name?' he said, 'Yahya' —which, as you know, means 'long life.' 'And what's his family name?' the guard asked. 'Ben Youssef' —the same name as the exiled sultan. The guard went inside and started calling out the detainees' names. When he called, 'Yahya Ben Youssef!' they shouted, 'Yahya! Yahya! Long live Ben Youssef!' (They meant the sultan.)

"For, of course, there was no detainee with that name. The guard went outside to look for the man who had delivered the basket, but he had vanished. It turned out the food basket had a bomb in it, and it exploded.

"After Independence, everyone pretended he had been the man who came to al-'Ader and said that the prisoner he was bringing food for was Yahya Ben Youssef, which meant 'Long live the exiled sultan.' Even some women claimed to have done it, just as everyone later claimed to have been the person who put the famous bomb in the central vegetable market in Casablanca. Mansour, when he set that bomb, saw that more Muslims than Nasara were entering the market. So he tried to neutralize the bomb, but it was too late. He escaped death, but he lost his forefinger.

"After that incident in al-'Ader, visits to prisoners were forbidden for several months. When they were allowed again I went to see Si Hmed and he said to me, 'Some detainees are short of money. Where are you staying now?' I said, 'At Si Abdelkader Ben Youssef's in Rabat.' He said, 'Go back there and tell him to send us some money.' (I can't remember how much it was now.) Even then, he thought that I might forget the exact amount by the time I got to Rabat, and so because visitors were watched by a guard and not allowed to give anything to the detainees or take anything from them, he later wrote the amount on a piece of paper and a German guard brought it to me in secret. Even though this guard served the French administration (which was unusual for a German), he was sympathetic to the Moroccans and friendly with the prisoners, because he was married to a Moroccan woman. I went to Rabat, got the money from Ben Youssef, brought it back to al-'Ader and gave it to the German's wife. She was named Fatna, may God mention her with good words if she's still alive or bless her soul if she is dead. She lived in a hut behind the prison and I used to stay overnight with her whenever we couldn't find transportation back to Casablanca."

In Sefrou, we had settled in the upstairs room that became my mother's after the distribution of her father's estate. When she went visiting my father in prison, she would leave us with her cousins. They lived outside the old walls of the city in a small house surrounded by fruit trees. In the early morning, the cousin's wife used to cook harira on a wood fire outside the kitchen. Her boys would climb a fig tree before the sun reached it, pick the figs while they were still cool, and bring them down in a basket. Then the family would all sit on the porch in front of the house and eat harira and figs for breakfast.

The summer was over. We were getting ready to enter school and my mother's old aunt Zineb came to her and said, "Is it true that you intend to enroll the girls at school?"

"Yes."

"Are you crazy? Who's going to buy them notebooks and pens?"

"The nationalists, aunt. They are taking care of us. They send us money every month."

"Send them to learn a craft and forget about school."

"I would do that if it were only up to me, but their father says every time I visit him, 'Take them to school,' and I've never gotten a letter from him in which he does not emphasize it."

"He spent his time having affairs with other women and spending money, then he went off to prison and now he decides to say school! What will a girl study, for heaven's sake and what for? A girl's destiny is marriage, pregnancy and breast-feeding, isn't it? One would think that they are going to learn that language you need to deal with *djinns*!"

"But my dear aunt, the Sultan Sidi Mohammed Ben Youssef himself has ordered the nationalists to send their girls to school. And every time I visit Si Hmed in prison he insists that I take them to school. I can't disobey him."

"Your husband's crazy and you're crazier than he is. You should be the one to decide. The proverb says, 'Show your friend the way, but if he refuses to see it, go your own way and leave him.'"

We did go to school, as my father had insisted. But before we began, there was always laundry day and bath day. The laundry and the bath came every week, but in those days before we started school, my mother made special occasions out of these weekly rituals.

On Tuesday evening, my mother gathered the laundry: our clothes, the cushion cases, the upholstery, the curtain from the door of our room, all the kitchen and floor rugs. She did not leave a single piece of cloth in the room. On Wednesday morning, she woke up before we did and made a wood fire in a large metal brazier outside in the courtyard. She filled the water boiler and put it on the brazier. She poured out the rest of the water she had kept overnight in two wood basins to close up their cracks, set them on two wood boxes, brought out the huge bundle of laundry and started sorting it: the head scarves, the whites, the colors, the black clothing, the rugs. She poured hot water and lye into one of the basins and washed the scarves and rinsed them; she hung them up on the roof because they dried more quickly than the heavy clothes, which she would hang there later.

In the courtyard she soaked the whites in the same basin in which she had washed the scarves and rubbed them with heavy-duty laundry soap on the scrubbing board, making a regular rhythmic sound. Then she took the washboard out of the basin and scrubbed everything again with both hands, taking each item separately and dipping it every now and then in the soapy water. She wrung them out and put them aside on a low table. Then she put the pile of colors to soak in the first basin, filled the second basin with hot water and shook the wrung-out whites into it. She lathered and rubbed each item with soap, and, bending far over, she worked the laundry through the soapy water, her hands going back and forth in a gentle motion. Then she wrung out all the items and threw them in the boiler. She poked the partly burned wood in the brazier to revive the fire, and every now and then she would stir the white laundry in the boiler with a long stick. When she got to the heavy upholstery, she gathered the fabric together, folded it lengthwise on a stick, and, with Grandma holding the other end tight, turned the stick clockwise, until not a drop of water was left in the fabric.

After the laundry had been washed, it still had to be taken to the roof, shaken, stretched on wires, turned over, collected and folded. The folding was the last stage. It was done at night on a sheet on the floor after my mother had stretched and pressed each item with her hands.

Laundry day was a gloomy day for me. The rooms were stripped bare, cooking in the house ceased, and the women and children stayed in traditional trousers and shirts which were basically underwear. Even though my mother allowed me to wash my dolls' clothes, I did not like laundry day, just as I did not like bath day. It gave me a feeling of strenuous effort and harsh life, which stayed with me all day until the evening call to prayer.

The day after laundry day was bath day. It began in the early hours of the morning. My mother put our clean clothes and towels into two bundles, one for her and one for my two sisters and me, and put the bath things into a metal bucket. We ate an early, improvised lunch and started out for the bathhouse before the men had left it. The bathhouse was around the corner on the next street, in the Adlouni neighborhood, and on the way Fatiha lagged behind and said that she didn't want to go to the bathhouse. My mother would first cajole her, and then she'd lose her patience:

"We'll sit in the brides' compartment, ma'am," she'd say, "and you'll get cold water with the little bucket, ma'am, and I'll wash you and treat you like a little bride, and give you oranges and sweet bread and, ma'am... For heaven's sake! Come here! May God never make me hear of your father's family and of the day I met them. Look at this fine lady!" indicating me with her eyes. "Look how *she* likes the bathhouse!"

But the truth is that I hated it just as much as Fatiha did. The very sight of the door of that bath house chilled my heart, but I went along anyway. Thursday after Thursday I carried the metal bucket and walked courageously at the head of our little procession. We were not the only children of our age who hated the bathhouse. I think that every Moroccan child in the traditional urban centers felt the same way, for we were scrubbed very hard, the water was too hot, and we had to sit there in the heat for hours while the grown-ups chatted and gossiped.

Even when we actually got to the bath, Fatiha would still resist. And we would wait until the last man walked out coughing and clearing his throat, his head covered with a towel under the hood of his djellabah, clutching the collar tightly to keep his neck warm. Then we rushed inside.

In the outer room of the bathhouse, we would all take off our clothes and put them in bundles, and leave them, our clean towels, and our clean clothes with the woman who was in charge of the bathhouse. Our mother would lead, as we pushed open the heavy wooden door and stepped into the darkness and steam of the first room, finding our way with difficulty. Our mother would stop there to fill with cold water the two wooden buckets she had been given in the outer room. We girls would go on through the middle room to an alcove that was called the brides' compartment. I would set down our metal bucket containing the bath things, and as our eyes became used to the dark we could see our mother coming with the heavy buckets. She would drag them to the innermost room, and I would leave my sisters in the brides' compartment and follow her. The buckets of cold water went to Yamna, the woman who ran the inside of the bathhouse. She would pour them into a large tub where hot water ran from a faucet. My mother would then place her empty buckets on a wooden platform and squat nearby to make sure that no one moved them from their place in line. I would stay beside her. Other women would come in, dragging their own wooden buckets of cold water to go through the same procedure, until about a dozen women were grouped around the platform. After a while the heat of the room would begin to affect them and one would urge the attendant on, saying, "Well? Well? Where's the hot water?"

"Be patient," the attendant would answer. "The tub isn't full yet. Has everybody brought her cold water?"

"Yes we have."

When the tub was full, the attendant ordered us to stay where we were. "I want no mess," she'd say. "No mess! I'll fill for everyone."

But no sooner did she stand up than all the women sprang up too, pushing and shouting: "Fill my bucket, Yamna!" "My bucket before hers." Then they would rush back into the middle room with steaming buckets and start washing themselves.

My mother would take her two buckets into the brides compartment, complaining as she came. "God! How aggressive the women of this neighborhood are! The way they talk and behave! Adlounis really have no manners!" She would set down her buckets of hot water and take our metal bucket into the first room to fill it with cold water. When she came back, she would drop two unpeeled oranges into the cold water and scrub herself. Someone would often comment on my mother's complaint: "Well, ma'am, those Adlouni women say it's their bathhouse."

"When the new one opens they can have this one all to themselves," my mother would retort. Then she would call to Yamna, "For the love of God's face, give me another empty bucket to fill with cold water so I can bathe the baby in it. The heat's going to kill her if I don't put her in some cold water."

"Okay, come and get it. But if we need that bucket you'll have to bring it right back. Tomorrow's Friday, you know, and everybody comes to the bathhouse today."

"I'll return it when I'm done with the baby," Mother would say.

My mother would bring the extra bucket full of cold water, put Naima in it to cool her down, and say to me, "Come Leila, let me wash you first so that you can look after your sisters while I wash."

She'd scrub my skin vigorously, wash my hair with *ghassoul* (a shampoo made of earth), and then start combing it. My hair was long, the bone comb was fine toothed, the water was hot, and she dug the comb into my scalp so hard that when she finally stopped and brought a towel I was seeing stars. She'd take me to the outer room, sit me on the mat of the platform, and order me to put on my clothes.

A little later she'd come out with Naima, put her next to me, dress her, and rush back to the middle room. Every time the door opened, Fatiha's screams came out with all the other noises and the steam, and made me realize how much my little sister was suffering. When my mother finally brought Fatiha out the attendant would say, "Why don't you take this child to a faqih and get her straightened out? Her behavior is too much."

"I've tried everything," my mother would answer in a discouraged tone. "I've even passed her under a camel. At El Ksiba I gave a camel owner twenty *rials* and said to him, 'Please pass this girl under your camel. They say it cures children's nervous problems.' And he did, but it didn't work."

Mother would leave us an orange and some sweet bread and say to me, "Watch your sisters, Leila! Don't let them go out in the street or uncover their heads, because they might catch a cold. Okay?" She'd turn back to the attendant: "For the love of God keep your eyes on them. I'll wash myself and come out. I won't be a minute." And she'd slip behind the heavy wet door that was standing ajar.

We would eat the bread and the orange and fall asleep on the mat. By the time our mother woke us up and we left the bathhouse, night had fallen and lights shone in the streets and shops. As soon as we got home, we'd drop the bucket and the bundle of towels and dirty clothes in the hall, go into our room and fall in our beds, too tired and sleepy to think of dinner.

The next morning at breakfast, Grandma would ask, "How was your bath?"

"A big mess," my mother would answer. "A crowd, not enough hot water, and those pushy Adlouni women. We came back and fell into bed, dead from exhaustion."

"How did Yamna behave?"

"She was okay. She gave me hot water, plus an extra empty bucket."

"She's learned her lesson, then. Not too long ago she was shouting at me about an extra bucket I had, and I said, 'Who do you think you are putting on such airs? Your job is to wait on people who need baths, and to pick up their shoes.'"

And Fatiha would say to my mother, "I peeked out at you when you were in that crowd by the hot-water tub, Mama, and I hoped that a djinn would appear and say to me, 'Make a wish.' And I would have said to him, 'I want an iron hook to take away all these women so my mother can have the hot-water tub all to herself."

Whenever Fatiha told that story, I would say, "You should have thought of telling the djinn to wait on us so Mother didn't have to work so hard."

Once Mother amused my grandmother with an extra piece of information: "That woman you know was there too," she said, "showing off as usual, wearing a caftan made of Khrib fabric, a silk belt, silk slippers and a scarf with Rabat embroidery."

"I hear," said Grandma, "that when she gets home she strips off the fine clothes and hangs them up. Who would wear a Khrib caftan in the public bath, for heaven's sake? It's crazy."

"Is that story about the woman who followed her home true?" asked my mother.

"Yes. That woman said to Yamna, 'I won't let her get away with showing off at the bath. I swear to God I'll follow her home and see if she still wears the fine clothes there, and then I'll come back and tell you.' The woman did go after her, then came back and told Yamna, 'I came upon her all of a sudden. The front door was open. I went in, knocked on another open door, lifted the curtain, went inside the room and there she was in rags that even a beggar wouldn't deign put on. And there was the Khrib caftan hanging on a nail.'"

"How did that woman explain her visit?" asked my mother.

"She said, 'We found this cup in the bathhouse and thought that it might be yours.'"

"'Women's stratagems caused me to flee; they use serpents as belts and scorpions as pins,' as Sidi Abdel-Rahman Al Majdoub, the old poet, says."

My sister Fatiha and I were enrolled in the girls' school, which stood on a strip of land between the river and the walls of the city. The row of classrooms had been built along one side of a narrow courtyard that was protected from the river by a high hedge of prickly pear bushes. The school faced the backs of old houses on the other side of the river, houses whose windows were decorated with the pointed arches of earlier times.

Fatiha and I went into the first grade and sat beside each other. The French teacher stood on a platform. She wore a black cloak and had short straight fair hair falling smoothly down. She took her hand out of the side slit of her buttoned cloak and started writing with chalk on the black board. She wrote "A" and I said, "A." Then she wrote "B" and I said, "B." She pointed at me and ordered, "Come here!" I went and stood beside her on the platform; she wrote "C" and asked, "And what's this?"

"C," I said.

She then wrote several words and I read them for her. Then, she took me to another room where there were much bigger girls. She spoke to the teacher and told me, "This is your class from now on."

There were four rows of pupils in that class. Two rows were second grade and two were third. I was one of the second-grade pupils and the teacher taught both grades alternately. I felt important staying in that room. Then the break bell rang and I ran out looking for my sister. I found her crying amidst a crowd of girls. When she saw me she stopped crying and said, "Didn't the Nasrani woman kill you?"

"No, no. She took me to the big girls' class." I answered.

"When she took you out the girl behind me told me, 'She's taking her out to kill her.'"

We started to walk alone to school every morning. There was no danger along the way, within the walls of the town. And in the narrow alleys were no cars, only pedestrians and donkeys. My mother had enrolled us in that school because my father had insisted on it. But presumably, she was not convinced this was the right path for us to follow, because she took us to learn caftan button-making as well. The making of caftan buttons was a craft of Sefrou women, Muslim as well as Jewish, who were said to be particularly skilled at it. The ancestors of the people of both these faiths had brought the craft to Morocco from Andalusia in the fifteenth century, when they were expelled together by the Spanish Christians. Jews lived in our community, as in every Moroccan community, not greatly loved but tolerated.

At the end of our alley, however, lived a Jewish grocer called Brahim, who had been a great friend of my grandfather and who had remained friendly with the family even after my grandfather had passed away. My grandmother would chat with him for a long time, then say afterwards, "There isn't the least trace of Jewishness in him. He sells me things on credit and is patient about payment. He never says, 'Where's my money?' even if I have had something for a year." Then she would confide in a serious tone, "I believe that he has secretly converted to Islam. When Bouazza's wedding procession passed in front of his store, he came out and threw candies on us. A Jew would never do that with Muslims. I'll cut my hand if he is not concealing his belief in Islam."

My grandmother knew how to exaggerate and embellish her narrations, how to fascinate and mesmerize the women of her audience. She would invite them to encourage her to continue by pausing from time to time, so that they would call out, "And then?" "Go on!" When we lived in El Ksiba I had always looked forward to her visits because of the wonderful stories she told and the fascinating way she told them.

So, during weekdays, I sat in the school classroom, which was decorated with delightful pictures of animals, to learn writing and reading and to memorize poems in Arabic and French. But on holidays and weekends I went with my sister Fatiha to the house of my mother's maternal cousin Tahra, a button mistress, to learn how to make caftan buttons. Her house was inside the town walls too, but it was rather far from our home. Tahra had a traditional three-room house. Her sister-in-law, an elderly divorced woman, occupied one of the rooms with her granddaughter, who was also learning how to make caftan buttons.

The button was composed of three layers. Tahra first made the body with a little paper square and a length of waxed silk thread. She folded the paper square into a triangle, moistened the top point of the triangle with saliva and twisted this tiny cube around a waxed silk thread. Then she curved the cube of paper and silk thread around a large steel nail, tied the whole thing with waxed thread, cut the thread and there was the completed body of the button!

She also spun the silk thread, steaming it in a boiling kettle so the spinning would not come undone. She measured the silk thread two and a half times around her hand and passed the thread back and forth between her forefinger and toe to make a hundred and twenty lengths of silk threads, the number necessary to make the buttons for one caftan. Then she cut one end of the silk thread she had passed between her forefinger and toe, tied it, put the hundred-and-twenty lengths of silk thread on my knee or Fatiha's, counted out one hundred and twenty button bodies, and put the button bodies on a tray that contained a needle and a regular nail for each of us. We were then taught to sew the silk thread over the button body, using tiny embroidery stitches that I remember to this day. Each girl's daily assignment was one hundred and twenty buttons. When we finished, Tahra cut the extra silk threads from our buttons, strung them together and arranged them into a set. She did all her teaching in the afternoons because in the mornings she cooked lunch, made bread, and cleaned the house.

I cannot remember how long it took us to become skilled in this craft. There were four of us apprentices in Tahra's house, which meant that we made no fewer than four sets of buttons a day for her profit. Even though she was our relative, we started to fear her and our mother began threatening us to get us to obey her: "Do this, or I'll tell Tahra." "Stop that, or I'll tell Tahra." Tahra did shake sticks from a quince tree at us, but she did not hit us. She only insulted and pinched us. She pinched so hard that it felt like an inoculation. It hurt a long time and left a bruise.

Later, for what reason I do not know, I was sent to a different button mistress, Fatma, my mother's paternal cousin. In her house I was the only apprentice. I went there holidays and weekends. She was the eldest of her siblings and lived next door to us with her parents, brothers and sisters. Fatma's family had another house in an orchard outside the town, where they lived in spring and summer. There, it was Fatma's practice to wake up at dawn, and fill earthen casks with water, straining it through a fine cloth. After that, she would make bread, cook lunch, and clean the house.

The house in that orchard had large rooms and traditional pointed windows looking out on the trees. This was unusual because the windows of traditional Moroccan houses almost always look inward onto the central courtyard. The rooms in Fatma's house also had smaller pointed windows, close to the high ceiling, and these were covered with a screen of carved plaster, through which the light came in beautiful patterns. In the courtyard, water ran from the faucet into a tub with a gentle sound, and there were doves that seemed to call out, "Mention Allah!" "Allah!" There were also sparrows that in our imagination seemed to tell a little story: "My husband bought me a head scarf, and I snatched one end of it and his second wife snatched the other and the scarf ripped, 'Crack!'"

When Fatma and her family returned to their house in town for the fall and winter, they would receive the neighborhood women in their courtyard, where they would gather and talk while working. They brought floor cushions along with their little work trays, and their silk thread. One of them would start the gossip and everyone would add a comment.

"Khaddouj! So, your brother-in-law is marrying again!"

"May it be the last time."

"He said his first wife was weird."

"Well, they do say she washed the charcoal."

"And what about the daughter of Bouklab?"

"That one lorded it over him, but he didn't mind because of her beauty."

"They say he beat her."

"Well, he came home in Ramadan one time and she said, 'He who dropped and lost his kif pipe will be helped by God to quit.' He was fasting, of course, and she was teasing him because he couldn't smoke. She said, 'Sunset is still far.' He smokes kif, you know. And so he beat her."

"Some say he divorced her because she was lazy. She didn't know any crafts and didn't do any housework."

"She was beautiful."

"Well, the proverb says: 'I'm fed up with your beauty, ma'am. When I go to sleep, I want a clean sheet to wrap around myself.'"

"He told her once, 'Cook us some harira tonight,' and she objected, saying, 'Harira is no easy matter. You have to buy me meat and, sir, you have to buy tomatoes and lentils and, sir, you have to buy me...' and she kept adding more and more until he said, 'I don't want any. You are going to make one sip cost me a rial.'"

"She was crazy and he was a kif addict. May God cut all the kif plants down. It has separated so many couples and destroyed so many men."

"That's right. Like Sa'dia. She was so beautiful, so young!"

"That one, poor thing, was destroyed by her mother-in-law, who gave the girl opium in a fig, can you believe it? That's worse than kif."

"No, no. It wasn't her mother-in-law, it was what her father did that destroyed her. Why would anyone give his daughter in marriage before she is old enough, and on condition that the husband not sleep with her until she reaches her legal majority?"

"Why indeed? Well, some people are still living in the Stone Age, it seems."

"So anyway, her mother-in-law gave Sa'dia that opium. Why? So her son could have intercourse with her and she'd be unable to resist. But when that girl woke up from the opium, something in her brain had gotten mixed up."

"What happened?"

"The mother-in-law had given her too much opium. When the girl woke up, the sight of her own blood gave her a terrible shock."

"Well, they both went to prison in the end for that, the mother and her son."

"Yes. Yes, I remember."

"Remember Britel's daughters? They were struck by the evil eye. Zineb, too: her husband robbed his best friend's safe and took her away to a foreign place."

"Sa'dia's case, though, was worse. These days she's neither with the living nor the dead."

"But Britel's daughters were really unlucky. There wasn't one man in town who didn't ask for their hands. Yahya Ben Hrazem wanted to marry Zineb..."

"The same Ben Hrazem who died in the Jewish quarter?"

"No, that one's first name is... Something else Ben Hrazem."

"But, the way that one died, I call upon God, one wouldn't wish it upon his worst enemy. The men were drinking wine at some Jewish place and Um Kulthum was singing on the gramophone, 'I swear that you are my wish, my desire.' They say that Ben Hrazem went out to the toilet, lost his balance, fell off the balcony into the courtyard, and died instantly. I call upon God! He died drunk, and in the Jewish quarter of all places."

"Troubles can be funny sometimes. They say his friends heard him fall and one went out to see what had happened. It was a long time before he came back and everyone shouted, 'Is he okay?' 'No,' the man shouted back, "he's not. Hrazem has fallen over for the last time.'"

"They were drunk."

A voice interrupted the women, calling from the end of the alley: "Mekouar is here!"

The women said, "Oh, it's the Fassi, the button dealer, announcing himself."

So they laid their trays on the ground and rushed out of the room. The button dealer set down his sack of silk thread and started collecting the buttons, calculating how many each woman had finished, paying for them, and delivering new colorful silk. Finally he stood up, put his sack over his shoulder, and walked away. We could hear his voice all the way from the next alley, mingled with the jingling of the bells of Baba, the water seller, who was singing his sad song:

I'm far from home and yet I have dear ones.
Oh dear ones, why do you forget those who are away?

And one of the women said, "That song of Baba's depresses me every time I hear it."

"The poor man's story is something else. They say he had a shop in Fez when disaster befell him. May God prevent disaster from striking us in this imperfect world! That man married his own daughter."

"The poor man! How could he do that? May God be kind to us!"

"He's from the Sahara, from the Dra'a. That's why he's black. They say he divorced his pregnant wife there, during the Year of Hunger, and that she went to Fez and worked as a maid with some family and that she gave birth to a girl. Days passed. Other days came. The mother died and the daughter stayed with that family in Fez. Destiny brought Baba to their alley, of all alleys, selling roasted chick-peas. And when he saw the girl, Satan put it into his mind to marry her. He asked for her hand and they married her to him according to God's tradition and that of the Prophet Mohammed, His Messenger.

46

"One day he asked her, 'Where are you from and how did you end up here?' She said, 'My family is from a village in the Dra'a valley. My mother was pregnant with me when she was divorced in the Year of Hunger, and she came here.' She said the name of the village and her mother's name, of course. 'My God! My God!' he gasped, and he began to moan and knock his head against the wall. Well, he went to a scholar of Islam who told him, 'Divorce her. Leave the town. Sell only water until the end of your days. Perhaps God will forgive you.'"

"There is no power and no strength save in God!" cried the women. They fell silent. Their needles became very active until someone knocked on the front door and a man's voice called out, "Make way!" It was my mother's uncle.

The neighborhood women covered their heads and turned their faces toward the wall, and the man's wife said, "Okay, pass now!"

He came in and looked away as he headed upstairs. Then my Aunt Hachmia started laughing and said, "I don't know why, but you all make me think of my cousin Zoubida, bless her soul! I bought a hairnet in El Ksiba. It was knitted out of black silk and its front edge was crescent-shaped, like the visor of a French soldier's hat, and decorated with shiny colored beads. My cousin saw it, bless her soul, and asked if I would sell it to her. I said, 'Okay.' Well, she bought it, wore it, and came downstairs right here to this courtyard, which would have told you this story itself if a courtyard could speak. My cousin sat down and started making her buttons and someone knocked on the front door. She slid the net back off her head and asked, 'Who is it?' She kept sliding that net back all day and asking, 'Who is it?' She knew only too well how ridiculous she looked in that shiny hat. Finally she put it in her chest and never took it out again. Bless her soul!"

"When Zoubida died," another woman joined in, "they asked Hussein why he wouldn't marry Hachmia, and he replied, 'Hachmia is right here. She's my cousin. I have her in the hood of my *burnous* like bread from the market. I want to look around a little, and if I don't find someone better I'll come back to her. Then, all I'll have to do is stretch my hand back to my hood and drag Hachmia out.'"

"Did I marry him?" said my aunt indignantly. "Of course I didn't. When he came asking for my hand, my mother said to him, 'Because of what you said long ago, I'd rather slaughter her by the drain than give her to you in marriage. How could you, puny little Hussein, compare my daughter to ordinary bread from the market?'"

"He has a sharp tongue, hasn't he? He loves using classical Arabic and quoting the Qur'an and the Hadith [the sayings of the Prophet]."

"My mother says," my aunt went on, "that he's been like that since childhood: 'God said...'. 'The Prophet said...' She says that my father,

47

bless his soul, was always telling him, 'You're misquoting!' and they would quarrel. She said that poor Grandmother, bless her soul, would then say to him, 'For God's sake, Hussein, stop meddling with God's and the Prophet's words!'"

My mother and grandmother did not join these gatherings in the courtyard of my mother's uncle, because they did not make buttons, but my grandmother once organized a picnic on the roof for her neighbors. Each woman brought something: sugar, tea and mint, bread, dried meat, black olives and butter from the farm. They grilled the meat over charcoal on skewers. But no sooner had they settled down to eat than someone knocked on the front door. Grandma leaned over the edge of the roof and shouted down into the courtyard, "Who is it?" "It's me," a woman's voice answered, and Grandma turned to the other women and whispered, "Oh my empty house! It's Lalla Khaddouj! Here she comes again using the name of the Prophet, begging as usual. Be quiet now, because if she hears you she'll come up."

Grandma went downstairs and opened the door and the woman entered saying, "You who love the Prophet! My Lord the Messenger of God is visiting your house."

"I ask God for His forgiveness," said Grandma. "Don't say that. My Lord the Messenger of God's rank is too great to visit my humble house. Come in, Lalla Khaddouj! Come in!"

"I'm his descendant and he who loves His descendants loves Him. Let me tell you. There's an orphan girl I know. She will soon marry and she needs two pillows stuffed with wool and a pure wool blanket from the city. Give them to me and I assure you a place in heaven."

"Come back tomorrow, Lalla Khaddouj, and I'll give you something."

"I'm not leaving unless you give me what I have asked for now. He who turns me out will anger the Prophet. It's a castle in heaven that I promise you. Remember, your daughter won her case in court and got her furniture back. Won't you give me some alms to thank God for that?"

My grandmother gave her two pillows and the woman went out talking loudly to herself. Grandma came back and one of the women said, "She uses the Prophet to twist people's arms. The beggar! The daughter of a beggar! 'The Prophet is visiting your house!' she says. May God forgive me for repeating her words. May the Prophet not plead for her, God willing. She uses her relationship to Him to twist people's arms. There's no bride and no orphan. She's just begging as usual and giving things to her daughter. People say that her daughter's house has mattresses stuffed this high, and all with wool."

"She always begs for wool."

"She never misses a wedding or a funeral. At weddings she shakes the tambourine and sings,

May God empower the sherifs,
sons of the messenger of God,
wherever they are.

"The descendants of the Prophet are venerated, but that does not have to be forced upon us. This business of 'I'm a sherif and you are common...' Aren't we all Muslims? The Messenger of God, may God's prayer and peace be upon Him, doesn't act like that."

My grandmother added, "And another big thing with her: she's always saying 'This girl is old,' 'This one is young,' just like the daughter of Mekki, who pretends that her daughters are young and other people's daughters are old."

"As if we were going to cook them! Why in heaven's name should people care about other people's daughters' ages?"

"An orphan bride, she says! The liar! There isn't a single wedding scheduled in town now."

"Except for Ali's engagement."

"Oh, that. Ali's family didn't mention it, but people have found out."

"His family's worried about his first wife."

"But the bride's family wants the entrance and the departure to be connected."

(I asked my mother what that meant, connecting entrance and departure, but she hushed me up, saying, "Be quiet! Don't speak when grown-ups are speaking." And I remained puzzled by that expression throughout the rest of my childhood. Actually, I had to wait until I grew up to find out by myself that it meant that a girl's family set the divorce of a man's first wife as a condition to his marrying their daughter.)

"Ali has waited all these years to take his revenge. Poor man! He wasted his youth with that woman from Fez who was his mother's age."

"His mother, Fatma Zerhounia, is responsible, may God forgive her. And greed plays a part in it, too. She went to Fez with her husband to get some gold teeth, and the Fassi dentist refused to be paid. Ali's mother had told them she was looking for a bride for her son, so the dentist took them to his house and presented a pretty young girl to them. She liked that girl and asked if they would marry her to her son, and they said, 'Of course.' But on the wedding day they changed that girl for another woman. They brought an ugly old maid. It was terrible.

The wedding became a funeral. Fatma Zerhounia made a big fuss. She screamed, 'They've changed her! That's not the one they showed me!' Ali's family had paid the dowry and had the marriage paper written and the wedding ceremony had started and the poor boy had spent all his life savings."

"Then why does Ali's family care about her feelings now?"

My grandmother prepared herself to make tea. She took off her apron and pulled down her skirts that were tucked up under her belt and over her black under-drawers.

A woman said to her, "Are you still wearing black *serwals*?"

"I complain to God, if I don't I become sick."

"Have you been to a fortune-teller about it?"

"What fortune-teller? The one that goes up and down the streets with her tray on her head shouting, 'Fortune-teller!' If she could tell people's fortunes she'd have done something about her own. In the old days, there was good fortune-telling, but that was when we could tell our own fortunes ourselves."

"How did you do it?" I asked.

"I'll tell you. Smail, the husband of Lalla Fatma, my mother's neighbor, had gone on a pilgrimage to Mecca. A year passed and he hadn't come back. And there was another woman whose baby had been sick for a long time. Lalla Fatma and the mother of the sick baby prepared two balls. I don't know what they made them with; I was young. And they went to the river and invited the demons to come out by throwing coriander seeds and carding needles into the water.

"That night when it was pitch dark they made a fire in a brazier in the courtyard. Without speaking a word, they went upstairs. Those who were afraid did not stay in the house. My mother, bless her soul, leaned over the edge of the balcony, dropped the first ball down into the burning brazier in the courtyard and said, 'That's the ball of the pilgrim. Is he dead or alive?' And we saw him going around the Ka'ba in Mecca and walking up and down the two holy rocks, Safa and Merwa. Then he faded away. My mother dropped the other ball into the brazier and said, 'This is the ball of the baby. How can he be cured of his illness?' And a little coffin appeared in the courtyard, and two men came and carried it away."

In the silence, my grandmother poured tea.

Another woman said to her, "Tell us the story of the female demon. (I mention the name of God the Beneficent, the Merciful) whom you saw combing her hair."

My grandmother laughed and said, "One night I couldn't sleep and I saw a woman demon and her daughters take shape in the room. She sat down on the ground, crossed her legs, and started combing her daughters' hair, one after the other. Then she combed her own. I had covered my head with the blanket and watched them through a hole in it. She braided her hair, tied her head scarf, picked the hairs out of the comb, rolled them around her forefinger and stuck them in the hole, in my eye."

They all laughed and a woman said, "That one had a sense of humor. But why don't demons appear to us these days?"

My grandmother explained, "In our day there was darkness at night, but today electricity is everywhere, in the streets, even in the toilets. Everywhere. So the demons are scared."

"Oh," said the woman to Grandma, "may you be protected from the evil eye. We all know you are blessed with special powers. You help women in labor, cure illness caused by the evil eye, stop witchcraft designed to obstruct marriage..."

"It all comes from God." said my grandmother humbly, "I just burn alum and African rue and say, 'The eye that strikes with evil intent, the blue eye, and the eye that has not prayed for the Prophet, may they be gouged out!' and 'May the evil eye of the young woman leave my patient and strike a riding animal instead! May that of the old woman strike garbage.' As for getting rid of witchcraft designed to prevent a marriage, it's just a matter of picking up some sticks at the Jewish graveyard, making a fire with them, heating water on it, and washing the girl's body with that water at the Moumen cave. God is my witness. I've never been to a fortune-teller, although I do ask Moulay Moukhtar to read that book, *Fate, as Foretold by the Prophets*, for me sometimes. It can tell you about your fortune."

It was the day of the picnic on the roof that I saw that aspect of my grandmother—the day when she and her neighbors chatted and told stories amidst the smells of mint tea and grilled meat.

A few days later she took every piece of furniture into the courtyard and started scrubbing the room, pouring buckets of water down the walls and in the corners, going in and out, singing all the time. She sang a song about gun shots within the city walls of Meknes, a song about Yankee soldiers who had come wearing military helmets and another song with words that I think I still remember:

I was sitting in my house in God's peace,
For the love of God my Lord!
When enemies came sneaking up on me,
For the love of God my Lord!
Do to them Lord, what they want to do to me,
For the love of God my Lord!

My grandmother's dinner that night consisted of mutton and turnips cooked with coriander leaves, with grilled peppers, tomato salad and some melon. Only the usual members of the family were there, but the food was so good that someone said, "Dinner in our honor."

"Just like my uncle did that time," said my mother.

They all laughed and my grandmother said, "Yes, I do remember. One day your uncle brought chicken, meat and fruit to his wife, the daughter of Mekki and said, 'Come here! Take these!' 'Who's coming for lunch?' she asked. 'The caid,' he replied. Well, she brought out her best dishes and trays. He prayed in the mosque, then returned and demanded, 'Is lunch ready?' 'Yes,' she said. 'And where's the caid?' she asked. 'Here he is!' he said, pointing at his chest.

After dinner my grandmother took the table away and started the ritual of making tea. The sugar container was so full that the lid was partly open. Inside were the large pieces of sugar she had cut earlier in the day with a steel cutter and a hammer. She had put the cut pieces into the container, saved the string and the white and blue papers that the sugar cone had been wrapped in, wrapped the smallest pieces of sugar in the white paper, neatly folded the blue one, rolled the string into a little ball and put everything away.

After tea she asked us riddles. We already knew them, but it didn't matter.

"What's the beautiful feathered lady who can neither be sold nor bought for any amount of money?"

"The eye!" we all shouted in one voice.

"Who are the two sisters, one for knocking and the other for parties and feasts?"

"The door-knocker ring and the ear ring!"

"What is 'There it is! There it is!' 'We can't see it!' 'It has crossed the railway, Mecca and the rivers of Chaouia, folded its arms and legs and slipped inside the house at the bottom of the alley!'"

"The crescent!"

"What is it that someone called out for at the garden gate and came in black and naked?"

"The eggplant!"

"What is it that someone called out for at the garden gate and it came in with a dent in its head?"

"The fig!"

During those evening get-togethers the grown-ups played games with us, the children. One game went like this: using both fists, we took turns placing them one on top of another to make a tower of fists. Then someone pointed to each fist from the bottom up and asked, "Whose dome is this?" and every time we gave the same answer in unison, "It's the Hdad's."

But then the person who was pointing got to the top fist and asked, "Whose dome is this?" We would answer, "It's the Sultan's."

"What's in it?" "Peaches and pomegranates."

"Where's my share?" "The cat ate it."

"Where's the cat?" "In the bushes."

"Where are the bushes?" "Burnt by fire."

"Where's the fire?" "Put out by water."

"Where's the water?" "The camel drank it."

"Where's the camel?" "The knife slaughtered it."

"Where's the knife?" "It's with the blacksmith."

"Where is the blacksmith?" "He went to fetch something and it fell on him. Oh, Mamma! His eyes are wide open." (He's dead.)

There was another game. "If a crow comes to you, give it one bag, and if two crows come to you, give them two bags as you gave one crow one bag, and if three crows come to you, give them three bags as you gave two crows two bags, as you gave one crow one bag..." and so on playing up and down with numbers and words. Each person took a turn until he or she made a mistake and had to drop out of the game. Whoever reached the highest number without any mistake was the winner.

A grown-up also would say to us during those evenings, "I'll tell you a little story: kebabs are in a small bowl; who's going to eat them?"

Each one of us tried to be the first to say, "Me!"

"I'll tell you a little story: grilled ground beef is in a small bowl, who's going to eat it?" "Me!"

"I'll tell you a little story: roasted chicken is in a small bowl, who's going to eat it?" "Me!"

And so on. Years later my youngest sister Souad joked about those games. She said, "The children of city people developed their egos at an early age."

"And a powerful imagination," I added.

After riddle games my grandmother often asked Moulay Moukhtar, my aunt Hachmia's husband, if he had his booklet of the *Fate, as Foretold by the Prophets*, with him. He would open the booklet at the index of women saints. She would close her eyes, put her finger on the index, and he would say, "You have chosen the fate of our lady Mary, the mother of Jesus." Then he would turn to the relevant page and read aloud what it said. That day he read this selection.

Fate, as Foretold by Our Mother Mary
May God be pleased with her

And it foretells blessing, good fortune and power in all things. Be informed, inquirer, that you can rely on God and should go ahead with the matter that you desire and about which you are inquiring, because it will bring you good fortune and complete satisfaction, *Inshallah*. However, you will be struck by a terrible and distressing affliction that will make you feel sorry for yourself. But God will save you. You will leave your husband and take him to court about your allowance. But this prediction may be wrong, because only God knows for certain. You will travel to another land and marry a disagreeable man who later will be attracted to another woman. You must wear an amulet and hold your tongue if you want to attain your desire. You will suffer a serious illness but you will recover from it completely. And there is a woman who hates you and wishes that you become ill and that you depart from your house. Protect yourself and you will be safe, *Inshallah* (if God so wills). So, praise God and give thanks to Him.

When Moulay Moukhtar was finished, my grandmother would say, "Yes, I know the woman who hates me and wishes me illness. It's the daughter of Mekki." But she never questioned the suggestion that though her husband had been dead for some years, she was going to be divorced and take her husband to court, or the part where it said that she would marry a second time, despite her lost teeth and gray hair.

I would say, "I want to know my fate too."

Moulay Moukhtar would go back to the index of the women saints and I would close my eyes and put my finger on the index and he would say, "It is our lady Aicha's lot. He would find the page and read,

Fate, as Foretold by our Mother Aicha
May God be pleased with her

And it foretells blessing, and good fortune. Be informed, inquirer, that you can rely on God and can go ahead with the matter that you desire and about which you are inquiring, because it will bring you good fortune and complete satisfaction, *Inshallah*. But you will always be sick because of the evil eye. You have a pleasant way of speaking. You may undergo the problems of polygamy, the strikes of demons, and the presence of a female demon. But you can protect yourself with a powerful amulet and you'll be safe from all the things you fear. This prediction may be wrong, because only God knows for certain. I see that you are envied and have many enemies. Conceal your affairs. Don't talk to anyone about them and pursue your desire. You'll attain it, *Inshallah.* So praise God and give thanks to Him.

When I would ask my grandmother to tell us the story, she would suggest, "Can he who's in love sleep?" She would say, "First pray for the prophet."

And we would say, "May God's prayer and peace be upon Him."

"I had a sickness of my eyes," she would begin. "My mother, bless her soul, had ground some peppermint and pressed the mint on my eyes and covered them with a cloth. It was after the afternoon prayer. We had finished dinner and were sitting in the courtyard, and I was lying with my head on my mother's lap. There were four of us: my mother, my brother Sidi Mohammed, bless his soul—he was one year younger than me—and Aicha, the wife of my half brother Abdelkader. She was beautiful. We were drinking tea and a pebble fell on the tray. My mother said, 'Oh! Where did that pebble come from? There is nothing above us but the sky.'"

Grandma would shiver and rub her hand on her arm as she always did when she got to that point of the story, and then exclaim, "God! I'm all pins and needles." She would go on: "When my mother said that, Aicha said to her, 'Lalla Tamou, tell us the story, "Can he who is in love sleep?"' and another pebble fell on the tray.

"The men, my father and Abdelkader were absent. They were irrigating in the orchard. Their turn to use the water was at night, and they always left home after dinner and worked in the orchard until morning. My mother stood up, with me in her arms, and said to Aicha, 'Come with me to my room tonight,' but Aicha refused and went to her own room upstairs. My mother carried me into our room and fastened the door with the wooden latch.

"In the morning when the men came home from the grove my mother told them about the pebbles falling. She had an idea how this could have happened. There lived in another house in the alley a handsome young man named Ba Sidi. He would cough whenever he passed our door and Aicha would rush to the front door with a small bucket and ask some little girl who would be going by to fill it for her from the faucet in the alley. My mother suspected that it was he who had come across the roofs that night, because he knew that the men were away irrigating.

"So, my father swore that Aicha would not stay married to his son, and Adelkader divorced her."

"Is the perfume-bottle story related to this one?" I would ask.

"No. That one happened much later to Fatma Boubker the wife of my brother Sidi Mohammed. He was a handsome, elegant man and definitely a playboy. He had a friend Driss, who was the mayor's nephew, but also was married to Amina, the mayor's daughter, so he was his son-in-law as well. Amina must have had a thing for Sidi Mohammed, because she was always sending her black maid to my mother to get his attention. 'Lalla Tamou,' the maid would say, 'my mistress has a stomach ache. What should she do?' 'She has a cold.' 'She has a headache.' And my poor mother would say, 'Tell her to drink thyme.' Or 'Tell her to drink cumin.' Or 'Tell her to mix the yolk of one egg and some flour and to rub the mixture on her temples and cover it with circles cut out of the blue paper in which the sugar cone is wrapped.'

"On Thursday evenings, my brother Sidi Mohammed used to get together with a group of friends at Driss' house. One day Amina sent her maid directly to the family shop with a message for Sidi Mohammed: 'Don't drink tea after dinner tonight,' went the message, 'because I am going to put a sleeping drug in it. When the guests fall asleep, I want to see you. Come, or I'll accuse you of attempting to seduce me.' The threat was a serious one because of the high rank of her father.

"So when her husband went out of town, she sent her maid to Sidi Mohammed, asking him to come to her, and he did. This happened every time her husband went out of town and it went on for months. But one day this was noticed by Ba Sidi, the man who seduced Aicha, my half brother's wife. Ba Sidi lived in the house opposite Driss, and from his tiny window he saw Sidi Mohammed go into Driss's house. So he told Driss what his wife was up to. 'Tell your wife that you're going out of town,' he said, 'and then come to my house and see for yourself.'

"Well, Driss took his advice and saw what my brother was doing. He decided to retaliate. He started sending the maid to Sidi Mohammed's wife Fatma Boubker with the message that he wanted to see her. Finally one day she said, 'All right. I'm going to stay for a while at my father's house in the qal'a [the old citadel near Sefrou]. Tell him to come tomorrow before the noon prayer to my aunt's house there. I'll be waiting.' That girl was really foolish."

"How can someone who is a fool figure out such complicated arrangements?" I wondered aloud.

56

"She was indeed foolish," my grandmother said firmly, then continued: "So, Driss went, carrying some food with him. It was a custom of the men to sit at the gate in the old wall around the *qal'a*, waiting for the noon prayer call. They saw the mayor's nephew approaching, carrying food with him. They asked, 'What's he coming here for? Maybe he's coming for some bad reason that will soil our honor.' Remember, Driss was famous for being a playboy. Some of the men followed him, saw him enter the house of Fatma Boubker's aunt, and went back to the gate. Along came Fatma Boubker's brother on his way back from work at the Sefrou post office. In those days, working at the post office was a great privilege. They told him, 'Driss has gone into the qal'a, and he answered, 'What do I care?'

"But when the brother got home and didn't find his sister, he asked his wife, who told him that Fatma Boubker had gone to have lunch with her aunt. He understood immediately what was going on because that aunt had a bad reputation. He rushed out, forced his way into his aunt's house and started searching. When he went upstairs, I call upon God, he found the two of them in the act.

"Well, Driss ran away and Fatma Boubker's brother dragged her by the hair down the staircase and through the alleys, unveiled and without her underwear. When he got her home he started beating her with a rope. After hearing what had happened, her father said to her, 'Get out of my house. You're not my daughter and I don't know you.' She went to her uncle's but they refused to let her in, and she was left out in the street until her father relented and said she could come home.

"My mother went to Fatma Boubker's father's house and found the woman vomiting blood. Even so, her father changed his mind again, and the family said that my mother could take her to our house.

"Several days later, people were talking on the street, but when my brother Sidi Mohamed, bless his soul, passed by and said, 'Peace be upon you!' they answered, 'And peace and God's mercy be upon you' and then lapsed into silence. Sidi Mohamed became suspicious and went to a close friend and said, 'When I speak to people who are talking on the street they stop talking.' And the friend told him the whole story and said that he had become the talk of the town in both Sefrou and the qal'a, and my brother said, 'It's a settlement of accounts by my former friend Driss, and my wife is a fool.'

"He went home and opened Fatma Boubker's chest of drawers to see if there would be some evidence in it, of her adultery. He found a perfume bottle and shouted to her, 'Who gave you this, whore?' He stepped out of the room, threw the bottle up to the roof and it fell and broke in the courtyard of a neighboring house. The master of *that* house was home and he said to his wife, 'I see that your lover is throwing a perfume bottle at you. I swear I will not stay married to you.'

"So there was an uproar in the neighbor's house too. The news instantly reached us and my mother went next door and said to the man of the house, 'It's only my son, he's had a fight with his wife and he threw that bottle.'

"My father, bless his soul, said, 'I swear by God in total faith, that Fatma Boubker will not stay in my house. She'll walk out with nothing for having done what is wrong.' And my brother divorced her.

"Well, Fatma Boubker went back to her father's house. But his heart had hardened again and he refused to let her in. Some relatives of hers said, 'She is a woman and we are not going to leave her in the street, and so they took her in.'

"Weeks later my brother, bless his soul, was in the family shop when the relative in whose house Fatma Boubker was staying came up behind him and hit him between his shoulders with some amulet. My brother said later that the effect of that blow on his resentment was like cleaning dirt from a sheet of glass.

"He came to me and fell on his face, crying. 'What's the matter, Sidi Mohammed?' I asked. 'I want to remarry her,' he said. 'The relative in whose house she is staying came to me in the shop today and said that they'll bring her home tomorrow.' 'Well and what about your father? Don't you remember he has sworn that she will not stay in his house?' 'I know,' he said, 'but there must be some way to get around that.'

"I went to my mother and told her what my brother wanted to do, and the next day two women relatives of Fatma Boubker brought her back to our house. My father was very old and had started praying at home except on Fridays. When they heard the muezzin call, 'There is no God but God,' and my father stood facing the direction of Mecca and said, 'God is greater,' the two women came in, fell on their knees, and threw their wool veils over him in a gesture to ask for pardon. He saw Fatma Boubker and understood what the women were after and said, 'If you had asked me to slaughter my son I'd have slaughtered him, but I cannot do what you ask. I have sworn an oath.' They said, 'You know that God will release you from the oath if you fast three days,' and he said, 'Very well. I will do it!' And that was that."

Stories. Grandmother. Buttons. And then there was school.

We were three friends at school: Hania, Fettouma and I. We always visited each other on holidays and shared our food at the school picnics on Wednesday afternoons in the olive groves by the Sidi Boumedian shrine. The school had moved to a larger building outside the town walls. On picnic afternoons everyone walked out in a long line two-by-two after entreating the principal to let us go by, shouting in the court-yard, "*Mademoiselle Béringuet! En promenade s'il vous plaît!*" I still don't understand why the pupils had to ask Miss Béringuet' permission to go on that outing, because the picnic was always scheduled for Wednes-days and the weather was usually sunny. But we had to.

Lalla Amina, who lived in our alley, was another friend of mine. She and I played hopscotch either in the alley or in the little square where the bakery stood. On holidays and weekends, we also played with a jump rope in the square in the morning while we waited for our bread. When the apprentice yelled, "Prayer be upon the Prophet!" we would know that the first batch of bread had been put into the oven. Sometimes the baker's boy took advantage of the fact that we were playing and not paying attention, and he would sneak away to deliver our bread to our homes. That way he would get a chunk of it for him-self as well as money to pay the baker. Then we would discover the scheme and get mad at the apprentice because my mother and Lalla Amina's step-mother would be cross with us for not bringing the bread ourselves.

On the second day of the feast of Eid al-Adha, Lalla Amina would bring her little brazier, a pot, meat and spices and join my two sisters and me on our roof. She would place all this next to our brazier and pot and meat and spices, and then each one of us would cook her own meal. We would taste the broth and advise each other: "Add more salt" or "That's too much salt."

Aside from the one picnic on the roof that I remember and the eve-nings she entertained in her room, my grandmother often gathered her neighbors for another sort of picnic by the shrine of Sidi Ali Bouserghine, the saint who is said to cure madness. This holy place is situated at the top of a mountain overlooking Sefrou.

A group of us, women and girls, would climb the mountain carry-ing blankets, trays, and baskets. Everything about that paved road to the shrine was familiar to us: the yellow mountain earth, the wildflow-ers, the thorny trees, the straying sheep in the fields.

From the top of the mountain, Sefrou shone white amid the green shrubbery. We could see our town through the ironwork in the little shrine window. One woman said, as if speaking of a living man, "Sefrou stands right in front of Sidi Bouserghine like a mirror in which he can see himself." And another woman added, "Like holy beads in his palm."

At my grandmother's picnic on the roof, people had said that there was no wedding in Sefrou at that time. However, an unexpected wed-ding did take place after a scandal that shook the community. A young couple had run away because their parents refused to allow them to marry. When they were caught, the parents were forced by convention to let them marry. The wedding was held in Zamghila, my school friend Hania's neighborhood, and Fettouma and I went with her to see the runaway bride. We found her in a room upstairs amid finely dressed women sitting on banquettes. She had lovely brown skin and was very pretty—or at least that's what I thought. The uninvited women onlookers outnumbered the guests.

The second wedding I attended in the town was that of the sister of my friend Lalla Amina. What was extraordinary about it was that the bride was poor and the bridegroom was the caid's son. Her father was the driver of the bus to Fez. He would leave at dawn and come back after the evening prayer, completely drunk every day. He was a descendant of the Prophet and yet he wasted his salary on wine.

As for the groom, even though his father no longer held the rank of caid, he was still called the caid's son and his father's house was still called the caid's house. What was also extraordinary about that wedding is that this former caid was celebrating the wedding of his two sons at the same time in what used to be the caid's residency and on this occasion, he had opened his door to the townspeople for the first time.

The brides' rooms were in one wing. All the women guests walked into that area first, carefully noting the items in the dowry of each bride, then proceeded to the main part of the house, a large, majestic-domed room that had pointed windows of colored glass looking onto the street, ceramic tiles, wood paneling, and a ceiling of carved plaster. The two brides, wearing green silk veils over their faces, sat on raised pillows placed in the middle of three banquettes; elaborately dressed women sat around them. A women's band sat on floor cushions on the rug beating drums, shaking a tambourine, and singing:

> My night! O my night!
> Lords! Bring her to me.
> O God! O my night!
> That Alaoui Sherifa
> O God! O my lord!
> Put her on the bed for me!
> O God! O my night!
> Water runs in brooks and I'm thirsty,
> O God! O my lord!
> Bread is on trays and I'm hungry,
> O God! O my lord!
> Lord! Bring her to me!

Each Friday afternoon during the two and half years that we lived in Sefrou, the public entertainer Harba came to Bab Al Maqam Square, and the townspeople gathered in a circle around him. The first time I went to one of his performances, he was still preparing himself when some people impatiently urged him to begin: "The war! Harba, do the war."

He ignored them and a man explained, "He leaves that to the end. If he starts with the war he'll break up the circle because he stamps his feet hard on the ground when he moves and that raises a lot of dust."

Then Harba announced, "I'll start with the bathhouse. Noufissa with the long, lank hair is in the middle room surrounded by wood buckets." He sat down, began mimicking the motions of pouring water on his head and sliding an imaginary comb from the top of his head slowly down to the ground, while making "tsk, tsk, tsk" sounds.

A baby girl on her sister's back started to cry and the audience shouted, "Take your sister out of here!" and the girl obediently left the circle.

Harba then stood up, pretended to tie his head in a scarf, and said, "As for Noufissa's neighbor, she went into the inner room, filled her bucket and dragged it to a dark corner." He sat down again, removed the imaginary scarf and made motions of hastily pouring a few cups of water from the bucket, looked around fearfully, then put the scarf back on, looked up at his audience and said, "Noufissa's neighbor is..." and everyone around him shouted, "Bald. She's bald!"

CHAPTER III
CASABLANCA

My memory still holds the faint traces of other images from these early times: one suffused with sadness and tears at leaving my friends in Sefrou, one an image of our first apartment on Suez Avenue in Casablanca, and finally a clearer image of another apartment on that avenue, where we lived until Morocco won its independence in 1956.

It was just after we moved to Casablanca that my mother and my grandfather reconciled. I remember the details clearly, for she told the story again and again:

"Robio, remember, was the one member of your father's family who was kind to me during the court case to get my dowry back. He and his mother Fettouma, his sister Fettouma, his maternal uncle Allal's wife Damia, and his maternal aunt Hadda came all the way to Casablanca to see your father. He was out of prison then and living with us in Casa. They stayed four days, or maybe six or eight. Before they left, Hadda said to me, 'Come with us; we'll help reconcile you with your father-in-law.' Someone asked your father what he thought about this idea and he said, 'It's up to her. I cannot force her to do that.' Your grandmother in Sefrou said to me, 'Go on, daughter, you should go, now that they ask you. For what they did to you, leave the punishment to God.' So I said to your father, 'Give me money for a bus ticket to Beni Mellal,' and he said, 'I don't have a franc and you know it.' Your grandmother gave me the money and I gave it to Robio, who bought the ticket."

In later years when Mother would tell me the story, I would say, "That wasn't a good idea to go to grandfather. From what you tell me, you weren't very wise."

"Well, I was obeying my mother. That's what upsets me. I obeyed my mother, and now my daughters don't obey me. It's true. Your father's family should have come to me, because they had done me wrong. Your grandmother should have told Robio's mother and the others, 'They treated her unjustly; they should come to her.'"

"Exactly."

"But you see, I was afraid of my mother. I was a married woman and I was still afraid of her. One time, my first husband had bought movie theater tickets and I even said to him, 'I need my mother's permission to go there with you.' Can you believe it?"

"If you'd been a bit wiser, Mother, you wouldn't have gone to my grandfather and his family. After all, they took your dowry and dragged you to court... ."

Mother would listen to me up to a point. Then she'd say, 'Enough! You're turning the knife in the wound. No more of that subject, now! It doesn't interest me... We didn't have a franc. It was my mother who gave me money to spend for food when Robio and the others came. Bouazza even bought a turkey with his pocket money and then said to me, 'Here, cook it for your guests. It'll make a meal or two.' Would I have gone to your grandfather and his family if it was not for my fear of my mother? What do I care about those people? Look at me now! Do I visit them now after what they did even after all that? Do I go to their houses?"

"Well, you have us with you now."

"No. No. No. It wasn't that. It was just because of my obedience to my mother... The bus stopped in Fini and I gave Robio enough money to buy me a sandwich, while his mother and the other women were calculating, 'How much money do you have left?' 'How much do *you* have left?' 'How much have you spent?' 'How much have *you* spent?' It was their first trip to Casablanca.

"We got to Beni Mellal and there they behaved as if they had never suggested that I come with them. 'Where will you go?' I became furious and said, 'Look! I'm going nowhere. I'm leaving.' And Damia said, 'She'll come with me.' She took me to her house, and her husband, bless his soul, bought meat and cut it up and put it on skewers, and she baked bread.

"Caid Haddou and his family lived on the first floor of Damia's house and they invited me for lunch, but she said, 'Don't go.' She was not on speaking terms with them. 'You're staying with me, don't talk to them.' 'But they're insisting,' I said. 'Come with me and let's reconcile you with them as well.' 'No!' she said. Then the caid's sister herself came to fetch me and I went with her. When I came back in the evening, Damia was very annoyed with me.

"The next day Hadda brought your grandfather over. Damia might have asked her to bring him. I don't know."

"Did Grandpa come? What did he say?" I asked.

"He said, 'Pardon us, daughter. We were out of our minds.' That's all."

"And he said everybody's sound judgment had returned?"

"No, he just took me to his house and I stayed there one day and then went back home."

"Did you really go? Did you enter their house?"

"Yes. I did," she said in a defiant tone. "Where else would I have gone? I stayed overnight and left the next morning."

Fatiha and I had to walk a long way from our second Suez Avenue apartment to reach our new school. It was called the Knowledge School and was in an ordinary house situated on an ordinary street among other houses. It had two stories and four rooms. The director and his wife lived in one of the rooms on the ground floor.

The Knowledge School was one of the Moroccan schools that had sprung up during those years in reaction to the French administration's attempt to do away with the Arabic language and replace it with French throughout the country's formal school system. Our school had been founded by its director, Mr. Moustapha Lahrizi, a man from the Casablanca region, who taught in it with his wife, Teacher Zoubida, a young woman from a traditional Fez family, who would lower her face veil in the classroom. They were helped in their mission by two distinguished young teachers. We were taught classical Arabic, except for one hour a week, when we had French lessons from a Moroccan.

When we first enrolled, we were given a reading test, using the illustrated reading book that was assigned in Lebanese primary schools of that time. They asked me to read a story called, "The Evil Rooster," the introduction to which I can still recite. "Do you see, Said, how this rooster lives by itself in a lonely cage? No one goes near it and no bird shares its food or water. It is the evil rooster that I mentioned to you the other day."

It was in that school that I learned the principles of Arabic, as pure as water from a spring, from teachers who loved the language and believed that to instill its principles in us was a religious and national duty.

As we walked to school in the Casablanca of those days, the city did not seem to bear any resemblance to its Spanish name, "white house"; on the contrary it was "the black house," as my mother called it in Arabic. It was a Casablanca where, on our way to school, we heard the sound of gunfire. We saw military patrols, with helmets and guns, wearing the resented French caps and flags, and sometimes we saw the dead bodies of Moroccan traitors and drunkards who had been shot down by the resistance fighters who were opposing the French.

Then we arrived at the classroom and were given a lesson in Arabic, on which we were supposed to concentrate all our energy. We were very young, and supposedly not affected by all these signs of national struggle, but we constantly carried in our hearts an anxiety about our nation. For we saw the effects of violence everywhere. And then our father, who had been out of prison only a few months, was detained again.

When I was older I asked my mother, "How did we end up in Casablanca? I don't remember how it happened or who helped us." She explained it at some length. "When your father had finished serving his sentence in al-'Ader, he wrote to me that he was getting out and gave me the exact date and hour. I took you girls with me on a bus to Kenitra, and a nationalist friend of his, Moulay Driss Bounani, drove us in his car to the prison at al-'Ader. When we arrived, we found your uncle Ma'ti there.

"The prison administration had told your father that he first had to go to Beni Mellal to sign a paper, and he went there with his brother and we went back to Sefrou with Moulay Driss. Then your father joined us. He stayed three days and announced, 'I'm going to Casablanca. The nationalists have found me a job there.' I had a big carved gold bracelet. I took it to Brahim the grocer to pawn it, may God mention him with good words if he is still alive. He was a Jew but he behaved like a Muslim."

A friend, a woman from Sefrou, my mother's hometown, who was listening to this story, interrupted her. "They, the Jews, were always making beer, may the angels forgive me, for mentioning beer. When they distilled figs to make it, we couldn't stand it. A nasty smell overpowered the town. They made it in their houses and sold it to Muslims and nobody could say, 'It's against Islamic law.' The French were ruling. The shopkeeper was a Jew, the mattress-maker was a Jew, the used-goods dealer was a Jew named Mouchy. That Mouchy passed through the streets calling out, 'Lalla, would you buy something? Lalla, would you make a bargain?'"

My mother said, "But by then he had already changed his way of addressing us. It used to be that when we heard his voice calling, 'Come buy something! Come, make a bargain!' my mother would say, "Listen to Mouchy. He says, 'Come!' and does not deign to be polite, and say Lalla to Muslim women."

My mother's friend concluded, "At their funerals the Jews always hired a female mourner. She would come and beat her hands on a low table and describe the dead person's character and his good deeds, and all the women cried and scratched their cheeks. For their weddings they hired a woman to do the ululation. The Jewish brides wore a pointed head dress called *hantouz* and tied long fake-wool braids in their hair."

My mother would always say to her friend, "Do you know where those fake braids come from? They are said to be the braids of our lord Noah's wife that a Jewish woman had stolen. She had cut them and tied them to her own hair."

And I would always tease my mother by smiling and asking her, "Did the Jews exist in our lord Noah's days?"

"I don't know." she would always answer, "We heard that story from our parents and they heard it from theirs. Only God knows."

Her friend would go on: "They fast only one day a year."

"You call that fasting?" retorted my mother. "They claim they are fasting but they eat seeds, and all day long they go, 'Tf, tf,' spitting the shells out."

I suggested, "Let's get back to our subject."

"Where was I?"

"You were talking about when you took your gold bracelet to Brahim the Jew, to pawn it."

"Oh yes. May God remind you to recite the *shahada* [the first duty of Islam] before your death! So, ma'am, I took that bracelet to him and he said, 'Look, Lalla, because of my friendship with your father, Sidi Serghini, I will not take any pawn from you.' He gave me the money and I gave it to your father and he went to Casablanca. Then your father wrote, 'Bring the furniture and come.' So we paid a truck owner and he drove us there. Your father had rented an apartment on Suez Avenue and was fixing it up for us. The painters were still there.

"The nationalists had found him a job in the teapot factory on Mediouna Road. The Nasara made a big mistake, you know. When they arrested the nationalists from all over Morocco and put them in jail together, they unintentionally arranged for them to meet and develop a system of cooperation in their nationalist activities. That could never have happened otherwise.

"Well, your father started working in the office of that teapot factory. He had one colleague there, Si Moustapha, an Algerian nationalist from Constantine who was exiled by the Nasara to Casablanca because of his nationalist activities in his own country.

"So, thanks to the connections he made when he was in al-'Ader jail, your father started getting guns and taking them to Hassan Laribi, a well-known shopkeeper in Beni Mellal who was originally from al-Sakiet al-Hamra in the Western Sahara. He and his fellow nationalists went in two cars; one carried the guns and the other drove ahead of it. One day the first car met a road block, so the driver turned around and both cars turned into the sands of a beach. The tires got stuck and the men had to dig the cars out with their bare hands. That's when your father lost his gold ring, and after your father was detained the second time, Ma'ti came to me and asked, 'Where's his gold ring? I didn't see it on his finger in the jail.'

"One of Hassan Laribi's employees found out about all these activities and told the Nasara. Your father came home from work one day and the news arrived: 'Hassan Laribi has been arrested and they have brought him to the central police station in Casablanca.' Beginning that night, your father went to bed with his clothes on. I asked. 'What do you think of Hassan Laribi?' and he said, 'He's a brave man, but torture will break him, torture!' How many people had they arrested? Let's see. About thirty. They tortured them about eight days. They kept on torturing them until they all confessed.

"Your father came home for lunch one afternoon and said, 'I have a bad feeling. I'm going to take a nap. Wake me up at two o'clock.' I said, 'Eat your lunch first,' and he said, 'No.' After I woke him, he started to go out, but when he reached the front door he stopped and came back... Oh, I forgot to say that I had fallen asleep too, and I saw myself in a dream swimming in a huge sea toward the shore, and when I had almost reached it a voice called from under the water. It said to me, 'Say a prayer for yourself and a prayer for the Sultan Ben Youssef,' and I put my head under the water, the way professional swimmers do, and began praying, 'God, help us and Ben Youssef through this crisis, God...' and a cold hand reached out of the water and tried to choke me. I sat up and saw that it was exactly two on the wall clock. I woke up your father and he walked as far as the front door, came back and bent over all of you and kissed you girls as you slept, then said to me, 'Be a woman!' and I asked myself, 'Is this it?'

"He left, and I started collecting the laundry and after a while the doorbell rang. I opened the door to find a man standing there. He spoke urgently to me: 'Look through the apartment and pick up every piece of paper that has writing on it and burn them all immediately.' I asked, 'Have they arrested him?' He nodded and left. I picked up every piece of paper, even the marriage contract, and went to fetch my Casablanca friends, Lalla Tam and Fatma, and we all went to the roof, burnt the papers and washed the roof. Two days later Si Moustapha came and told me what had happened

"We were in the office when three jeeps arrived," he said. "One was carrying a prisoner, Hassan Laribi, covered with a military blanket, and the other two were filled with soldiers armed to the teeth. The soldiers got out and rang the bell and I opened the door. One of them asked, 'Is Bouzid here?' I pretended that I didn't understand; I said, 'Eh...?' He repeated impatiently, 'Is Bouzid here?' I asked, 'Who wants him?' and Si Hmed said from inside the office, 'Yes, he is.' The Nasrani went in and handed him his jacket from a hanger and he put it on and went out with the soldiers. I followed them to the factory gate. All the other soldiers were now standing around the jeep guarding the prisoner under the blanket. One of them uncovered the man's face so that he could see and confirm that their newest prisoner was Si Hmed. 'Well,' Si Moustapha said, 'I saw *his* face. It was Hassan Laribi.'"

My mother continued, "We, Lalla Tam, Fatma and I went in search of your father from one police station to another. I'd leave them outside and go in and Muslim policemen would ask, 'What do you want?' 'My husband,' I'd answer. 'Why are you looking for him?' 'He went out two days ago and hasn't come back.' 'Does he gamble?' 'No'. 'Does he drink?' 'No.' 'Is he a nationalist?' 'I don't know.' And they'd send me to another station.

"Finally, at one of the police stations I came upon a black policeman, a huge man, built like a cask. May God's prayer be on the Prophet, he was Muslim. I said, 'Good morning, sir!' 'Good morning ma'am!' 'My husband went out and hasn't come back and I have three little girls.' He said, 'Listen, Lalla, if you know that he's a nationalist, there's no need to waste more of your time here. Nationalists are taken to a special station. Go there, but don't say that you talked to me. Think of what you'll answer if they ask you who sent you there.' 'I'll say I've searched in every station until I got to this one.' And the black policeman began to give me directions. I stopped him and said, 'I'm not from this city, sir. Come here, Lalla Tam!' She came in, and he explained to her how to get to that other police station and we went there.

"Again, my two friends stayed outside and I went in. 'What do you want?' I explained and the policeman asked, 'Is he a nationalist?' 'I have no idea. I have looked in every station until I got here. I have been looking for him everywhere. I have been looking for days.' 'What's his name?' 'Si Hmed Bouzid.' He looked at a list and said, 'We have arrested him but he isn't here. He is at the military prison.' So, we headed toward the military prison. There we found women standing in groups, some of them crying and others telling their stories. Lalla Tam and Fatma and I each went to a different group and asked. 'What does one do here, Lalla? We only found out today that our detainee is here and we don't know what to do.' 'Did they give you his number?' 'No.' 'Then go and buy some food, and try to deliver it by giving his name to a guard and see what happens.'

"I went away and bought bread, cheese and cigarettes. I tied them up in my apron and put the bundle on the pavement in a line with the other women's baskets. A Nasrani guard came. He looked at the baskets and pointed at my bundle with his machine gun and demanded, 'Whose is this?' 'It's mine,' I replied. 'What's your detainee's name?' 'Si Hmed Bouzid.' 'Where's the number?' 'I've no number. I went to some police stations and at one of them they told me that he's here.' He took the bundle inside the prison, brought the apron back to me, and I knew that he was there. So, then I began taking food to that prison every day. But one day they wouldn't let me leave any. So I started going there every day again and again from seven o'clock in the morning to seven at night. I was hoping they'd change their minds and take the food inside. All during those days I kept taking food and they kept refusing to deliver it.

"In that prison there were also inmates who had been convicted of misdemeanors. One of them took the nationalists' food into the prison. He stole some of it, but he brought out news for us. One day he came out and said, 'The jeep that's coming out now has three nationalists in it. Two are dead and one is dying.' 'Who are they?' the women asked. 'I don't know. They're covered up.'

"A jeep drove out with three guards in it. It stopped and I approached it and asked, 'Please, why is my food not allowed in?' 'What's your prisoner's name?' 'Si Hmed Bouzid.' 'Don't say that name,' one of them said, and the other one added, 'because he's dead. We've sent his body to the hospital to be prepared.' 'You had no right to do that. I've been here all day. Why didn't you tell me?' The third one said, 'We haven't buried him yet. Go away now and come back at three.'

"I went back home and didn't tell you girls anything about what he had said. At three I went back to the jail with Lalla Tam and Fatma and Fatiha. I said to my friends, 'Wait for me here. If I don't come out before the end of the day, then I have been arrested.' The guard opened the prison gate and I went in with Fatiha. I found the food the women had brought earlier in the day in a mess in a courtyard. Some of the inmates, the ones who were in jail for misdemeanors, were searching it for hidden articles. The prison guards let the inmates search because they were starving. The prisoners would poke at the baskets as if searching them, then manage to eat some of the food. They would cut a whole chicken in two to see if there were anything inside.

"A Nasrani came and led Fatiha and me up a staircase to the third floor, made three turns along some corridors and took us into an office where another Nasrani was sitting. He was obviously the director of the prison. His office was here," she gestured, "and one of the cells was there, facing it, and the wall of that office was covered with keys hanging on hooks.

"Oh! I forgot to tell you something. May you never be afflicted with distress, daughter, and may you never witness it. When they told me he was dead and I went back home, Si Moustapha came and I told him the news. He said, 'Let us pray to God that he did not die under torture. Give me the booklet with your family registrations. I'll have to put the girls in another school.'

"The Nasrani in the room where Fatiha and I were taken asked me, 'Are you his wife?' 'Yes' I said. He repeated the question three times. I said 'yes' every time. He stood up, walked around, opened the cell facing into the room and brought out a man whose head and face were wrapped in bandages so that only his eyes, nose and mouth could be seen. His lower lids were turned over. Poor man, I thought. Later I found out that they'd hung him up by his feet with his head in the toilet. He came over to us and bent over Fatiha and kissed her. 'Si Hmed?' I asked. 'Yes,' he answered. 'Be strong. Don't cry, because that is the situation they love the most.'

"The Nasara started talking to him. He turned to me and said, 'Do you know what they're saying?' 'No, I don't.' 'They are saying that you went to the mayor of Sefrou with a complaint and that you have hired a lawyer.' 'But I haven't gone to anyone with any complaint and I haven't hired anybody.'

"The Nasrani who was sitting down when we came into the office turned and spoke to me in Arabic. I was startled, because he spoke it as if he were a Muslim. He said, 'Don't tell me that you didn't go to Mayor Bakkay. Look! Fatma, daughter of Serghini from Sefrou, you lived in Taksebt, on the Alley of Rahma Al Khanguia, number seven. Now you live on Suez Avenue, number twenty. Even the number of your husband's cell in the complaint is correct.'

"He said that the lawyer had come and told him that I had hired him. I said, 'I didn't.' The Nasrani said to your father, 'Talk to her.' And Si Hmed said to me, 'If you made a complaint, say so. Don't be afraid. It is the lawyer who brought me back here from the hospital and demanded that you be allowed to see me.' I insisted, 'I didn't.' And the Nasrani said to him, 'Take her into the next room and talk to her.' Your father took me there and said, 'If you made a complaint say so.' I said, 'I didn't.' He went back and said to the Nasrani, 'She denies it.' The Nasrani said, 'Impossible.' And Si Hmed replied, 'Look! Why don't you send a public caller through the streets of Casablanca to shout, "Who has hired a lawyer to defend Bouzid?" Because she says that she didn't.'"

I interrupted then. "He was still exuberant then, hot-headed, I think. Wasn't he, Mother? He hadn't yet been tortured by the Moroccan police like he was later."

When I said that I was thinking of a day in 1969, when I returned home from eighteen months in London, and my father came to meet me at the airport. A Moroccan policeman at the airport had spoken to me harshly and I had replied in the same way. After all, was I not returning from the land of democracy? And then I saw him, my poor father with his emaciated body, moving backwards away from me, looking around in terror and anxiously waving his stretched out hand up and down at me, as if to say, "Quiet! Quiet!" I felt a chill. I realized at that moment the extent of the torture he must have suffered in police stations when he was arrested again after Independence this time by his own countrymen and accused of conspiracy against the monarchy.

70

Of those first nationalist days, my mother spoke again and again. "I said to your father, 'They are refusing to accept the food I bring.' And Si Hmed would reply, 'Bring it only twice a week but more of it each time.'

"So, the guards took him out and one Nasrani left the office and the other one stayed. He took off his jacket, rolled up his shirt sleeves and started stretching his arms and flexing his muscles — to intimidate me, I guess. Then he asked, 'Who's supporting you and your daughters?' I replied, 'I sold my own property that I inherited to provide for my family.' He demanded, 'Do the nationalists give you money?' 'What do you mean by nationalists?' I asked. 'I don't know this word and don't even know why my husband is here.' 'Do you know his friends in Beni Mellal?' I told him, 'We're not like you French people. We don't sit at the table with men and so we don't know our husbands' friends.'

"I went out and found the women relatives of the detainees and my two friends waiting for me outside the prison gate. As soon as they saw me, they all rushed to me and asked, 'Is he dead, Lalla?' 'No,' I said. Then I went to Si Moustapha's house. His wife was cooking lunch, working the bellows to keep the fire going in a brazier. Her husband was walking back and forth in the room with his hands behind his back. I told him what had happened, and he said, 'Do you remember you gave me your family booklet? Well, we took the information from it and sent a woman who looks very different from the booklet description of you (she was tall and tattooed) to deliver the complaint and hire a lawyer. We did that to send the message to the French that there are still nationalists out here.'

"Several weeks later, I put the food basket on the ground at the prison gate and a guard came. 'Won't you take my basket?' I asked. 'I've spoken to the director and he said that it will be allowed into the prison.' 'It will not,' he answered, 'no matter whom you talk to.' Another guard came and hit me in the back with the butt of his machine gun. I was pregnant. A third man, a Moroccan, came and asked, 'You want news of Bouzid?' 'Yes.' 'Wait for me.' He went inside the prison.

"When he came out, two women rushed to him and I followed them. One of these women said to him, 'Well sir. What's the news?' The guard said, 'What do you want me to tell you, Lalla? It was your brother who denounced your husband because the Nasara bribed him.' The prisoner's sister began to slap her cheeks and lament: 'Oh my mother! Oh my brother! You who used to feed this brother-in-law of yours. He has sold you to the Nasara!' But the wife shook her head, 'My brother would not have done that,' she said, and the guard answered, 'Did you have couscous with chick-peas and raisins for dinner last Friday?' The detainee's sister said, 'Yes, we did.' 'That Friday night when you had that meal, your brother learned that the guests were nationalists and he informed the Nasara.'

"The two poor women then went away and I asked the guard, 'What about me? What can you tell me?' He said, 'They have stripped him to his underwear and beat him every day for the last month on his breast and back. When he bleeds they turn him upside down, strapped to a board, but he still denies the charge against him. They asked him. "What about that person who denounced you?" And he said, "He has been my enemy since our school days. He accuses me falsely." Now if God helps him and if he sticks to his word they'll release him in a week. Tomorrow, wait for me here with your food and I'll take it inside.' 'What's your name,' I asked, 'and where do you live?' 'Hussein' he said. 'And I live on Ouled Zian, at such and such a number.'

"I went immediately to Si Moustapha and told him what the guard had reported to me about Si Hmed. He asked if the man had given me his name and address. I said, 'Yes,' and I mentioned them to him. And they went to Hussein that night. They gave him money and told him, 'Give it to the fellows who beat him so that they won't hit him so hard. Are they Moroccans?' 'They are.' 'Do they take bribery?' 'They do.' 'How many are there?' 'Two.'

"The guards did beat the inmates really hard. I swear by God, when they took me inside, I saw one of them in a white garment all stained with blood, like a butcher."

All during those bad times, we girls went back and forth to school. Naima now came with me and Fatiha, so my mother was relieved of her care. She could go to the jail daily, burdened only by her basket and her pregnant belly. We went along with her every now and then, probably on holidays. I remember the gate of Ghbila, the main prison in Casablanca, and the sight of the prisoners accused of misdemeanors. They wore harsh dark garments that looked as though they had been made out of military blankets. They were country people and had very brown skins from working in the sun, and black hair. These were the men who laid our food baskets on boards and carried them inside the prison.

I remember a quarrel between my mother and a guard about a cone of sugar that had been stolen and did not get to my father. I remember the long, narrow visitors' room, where the families of the prisoners would stand behind a wire fence, looking across the central corridor to the other side of the room, where the prisoners themselves were kept behind a second wire fence. And in the corridor between the fences, between the prisoners and their families, a French guard walked back and forth, carrying a big bunch of clanking black keys.

I remember the gate of another Casablanca prison in an isolated factory area, the walls of which are linked in my memory with the Berlin Wall. They were high walls, topped with thick strands of barbed wire, and in front of them stood an extremely blond, fair-skinned sentry. The sight of him in that forbidding setting convinced me that he was a German soldier in Hitler's army.

I have no idea why that "German" is linked with the image of my father lying unconscious in a jeep, his face covered with blood from a wound in his head, as he was driven out of that prison gate to a hospital. Nor do I know why all this is linked with the idea of death and the sound of one word, in different intonations: "Dead." "Dead?" "Dead!"

But my father did not die. The French withdrew in 1956. Morocco was granted its independence. And with the dawn of this new era events moved quickly. All nationalist prisoners were released and the sultan returned to Rabat from his four-year exile, to the great joy of his people. No sooner did our father leave jail than he was appointed mayor of Beni Mellal.

In that memorable year, 1956, there was another happy event. Just before my father was released from prison, I was awakened by a commotion in our apartment. I found the door of my mother's room closed and then saw my grandmother going in with a steaming basin and my uncle Bouazza standing in the narrow hall with an expectant air. Then a woman I didn't know came out of the room. She was an elderly Moroccan with short hair and European clothes. My uncle asked her, "What's the news?"

"It's a girl," she replied.

He went in and took me with him. I bent over the little bed that my mother had bought, and I saw a baby with closed eyes and a lot of soft, dark hair.

I probably did not sleep the rest of the night. The next day when Fatiha and I were proceeding slowly home from school as usual, all of a sudden I stopped and jumped in surprise, remembering, and exclaimed, "Sister!"

"What?"

"The baby!"

And we ran and ran, despite our heavy bags, until we reached home and stood beside the little bed. We bent over it, looking carefully at our baby sister and putting our fingers in her amazingly tight little fist, our new sister who came with Moroccan Independence.

The family was wondering what to call the new baby.

"Souad," I said, for Souad means one who has good fortune and also brings it.

"Yes, yes," they agreed. "She's brought a lot of good fortune: Independence, the return of Ben Youssef, the release of her father from jail, and a new job for him—mayor. She's fortunate indeed."

When women asked, "Who named the baby?" my mother replied, "Leila, ma'am, Leila did."

Later I asked her, "And who named *me*?"

"Your father," she said. "He called you after Leila Mourad, that Egyptian singer. His mother wanted him to call you Fatima and I wanted you to be named Fadila because you were born on Qadr Eve (the night in Ramadan when the Qur'an is said to have first been revealed to Mohammed). I was making sweets. I had been fasting. I refused to break my fast even though the water had started coming from me. I vowed, 'I won't break my fast until the baby comes out.' Lalla Khadija the midwife, bless her soul, came to stay overnight with me, and you were born on the Qadr Eve."

When I was older I asked my mother, "What's the story of that wound on my father's head?" At the time it happened, I knew that the French had wounded him severely on the top of his head. After Independence I saw the scar, thick and branching, as I sat behind him in our car, and I thought, "Because of that, God is able to forgive all your sins."

My mother told me, "He got that wound in the military prison in Casablanca. We lived in the apartment building overlooking the al-Manjra fabric market. The nationalists had warned the shopkeepers against selling French goods, including fabrics, of course, but a salesman in that market still sold them. So the nationalists put a bomb under a cane chair in front of his shop and then went in and shot him. The police came, ordered all the shop keepers to go out and leave their shops open, then tried to carry the dead man out, and the grenade exploded and killed them.

"That evening your father was at a meeting in a garage with his nationalist friends. The curfew bugle was blown at seven o'clock and he ran out. The police blew their whistles for him to stop, but he turned the corner, entered our building quickly, and slammed the door, and they turned and entered the next building. They knocked on an apartment door there, were admitted and asked a man whom they found inside to stand up. They felt his chest to see if he had been running, and asked him, 'When did you come back home?' 'At six,' he answered.

"It was that man's wife who told me all this on the roof. The Nasara started to search the apartment buildings around the market, looking for the people who killed the salesman and planted the bomb. In our apartment your father had guns and photographs of the sultan. He took the guns from the cupboard where he had hidden them and tied them to my waist with a large scarf. Then I lay down in bed and covered myself with a blanket.

"The doorbell rang. Your father opened the door and the Nasara came in. They found a rolled rug standing in a corner of the hallway and one of them pushed it over with the butt of his machine gun, then stepped on it to see if someone was hiding inside. He came into the room, turned the light on, and I could see the photographs of the sultan scattered on the floor. They had been hidden in the cupboard also and fell down when your father took out the guns. The soldiers didn't see them. They just kicked the mattresses and went out. It was then that I miscarried the twin boys.

"Then ten guerrilla fighters were arrested in Rabat and these men were brought to prison in Casablanca. The Nasara began to torture them as punishment and also for information about other Moroccans who had worked with the group. They increased the torture when they saw that nationalist activity had stopped in Rabat, assuming that these ten prisoners had been responsible for all the resistance operations there.

"Your father said to me, 'You must to go to Si Abdelkader Ben Youssef in Rabat and tell him that he and his group have to carry out some operation to convince the Nasara that these ten men were not responsible for all the operations in Rabat so that this torture will stop!' He began to name the ten men but I said, 'I will not remember all of them. Write them down for me.' 'But the police are searching people everywhere,' he warned. He wrote the names on a piece of paper that I hid in my clothes and I got on a bus and arrived safely in Rabat. I gave your father's message and the paper to Si Abdelkader's wife and she gave them to her husband. He said, 'Tell her to go back and let him know we have no guns. Tell him that his unit must send us some and then we will act.'

"I took the bus back to Casablanca and went straight to the teapot factory. The guard called Si Hmed and he came out. We went home and he gave me the guns, the same ones that were in the cupboard. He tied them to me as he did before and asked, 'What will you say if they catch you?' 'I'll say that a man came to me at the bus station, threatened me with a gun and ordered me to carry them to Rabat, where he would meet me and take them back.'

"I went to the bus station, but the bus to Rabat was full, so I had to take the train. I got to Rabat and went out of the station by the back entrance. Moroccans were forbidden to use the main entrance. I got to the street and saw a group of police walking toward me. I was terrified, but they entered a restaurant. May they eat bitter fruit, I cursed them.

"I went to the medina and found the rug market under surveillance by soldiers everywhere. I sneaked around the corner into an alley and hid behind a door that was ajar and stayed there until the soldiers went away. Then I resumed my walk through the medina to Si Abdelkader's house, trying to look as if I was casually walking around.

"It was then that your father was arrested and put in prison for taking guns to Hassan Laribi. I have told you about this before. There, the Nasrani guard took in everybody else's food and left mine. When I pointed to the basket and asked, 'What about this one?' he said, 'This one's owner is a pig.' Then other guards brought out your father's underwear soaked in blood with pieces of human skin stuck to it. Two guards had whipped him on his belly and breast, one on his right side and the other on his left. They stripped the other detainees naked to beat them, but your father had refused to take off his underwear. Later Si Moustapha brought me a dozen pants and shirts to take to him. It was during one of these torturing sessions that your father was hit on the top of the head with a club.

"That's the story of the wound. Your father almost died from it. They tortured him when they interrogated him. 'Free, fair, brotherly' France wounded him in the head because he was asking for freedom for his country."

Here I would break in, and tell my mother, "They're all the same. The Western countries, I mean. They preach lofty principles in fine language as long as these principles serve their purposes."

"What do you mean by 'Western countries,' my dear? Do you mean the Nasara, or what?"

"Yes. But there's another word that blacks in the United States use: 'Whites.' 'Nasara', 'the West,' 'Whites.' They all mean the same thing. Isn't the England that led the Crusades against Palestine in the Middle Ages the same England that wove the conspiracy to destroy Palestine in the twentieth century?"

My mother would look at me and wait until I had finished, then go on with her story.

"Then they transferred your father to the Ghbila prison. And when the Sultan returned they started allowing visits without permits. One day I went to the prison and a Moroccan guard said to me, 'Your husband wants you to bring him some harira.' I went home and cooked some, then took it to the prison in a covered white tin bucket. I put the bucket on the ground and the guard asked, 'Where's my share?' 'Help yourself,' I replied, and he poured some harira for himself, then took me to a room, went out, and came back with your father. He left us there sitting on two chairs. Your father asked, 'What does the man who gave you visitors' permits for this prison look like?' 'He's a young Moroccan,' I said, 'with smallpox scars on his face.' 'Go to him tomorrow. Tell him the prisoners have sent you, that they want to know why only some prisoners have been released.'

"The next day, early in the morning I walked all the way from Suez Avenue to the medina where the permit office was, with my pregnant belly sticking out. I found the gate closed and waited. When the man arrived he asked, 'What're you doing here? Don't you know that permits are not needed any more?' 'I know. May God protect you. I came because I want to talk to you.' He opened the door to his office and then the window. I said, 'The prisoners have sent me. I described you to him and he said that you were one of their men.' I continued, 'Do you know what I compare you to? A bee. It stings and gives honey. Others in your profession are like wasps. They sting and give nothing.' 'Wow!' he said. 'I have never in my life heard anything like that. Come on in!'

"I went in, sat down, and said, 'The prisoners want to know why only some of them have been freed. What's the reason?' He replied, 'I'll tell you the reason, Lalla, for the sake of your sweet tongue. Tell them that the Nasara have held a meeting to examine the files of each one of the prisoners, and made note of their sentences. They have decided to free those who have light sentences first. Tell them not to worry, that Sultan Ben Youssef is back and he'll free them all.'

"When Ben Youssef first came back he appealed to the nationalists not to undertake any vengeful act against traitors. But one man had sworn to kill his neighborhood official for having been too cruel to his fellow country people, and so he did, and the authorities caught him. The young man said to me, 'Tell the prisoners that fellow is in the same prison with them, and that the Nasara have decided to murder him.'

"I went back to the prison and told all of this to your father, who said, 'They've brought the man here all right. We know about him. Now tomorrow, bring me a woman's djellaba and a face veil.'

"The next day they let us visitors in, counted us and wrote the number on a board. Then, in the courtyard a misdemeanor prisoner hit another one with a bucket. That one asked, 'Are you crazy? What have I done to you?' They started fighting and insulting each other and a guard came. 'What's all this about?' 'He hit me with a bucket. Didn't you see him? I didn't do anything to him, I was just going by him quietly and he picked up the bucket and hit me.'

"I was at the back of the crowd, and while this ruckus was going on, I saw one of the visitors erase a number on the board and write another one instead. That's how they got the man out. The guards didn't notice what was going on because those two were fighting. So you see, even some of the misdemeanor prisoners in that jail contributed to our struggle. That's an example. Oh! I forgot. I had brought sunglasses for the condemned man, too, because he had struggled with the official before killing him and the latter had scratched him on the face.

"When we got to the visitors' room, they had opened the gates in the two wire barriers that separated the detainees from the visitors. The prisoners had come to the visitors' side and the guards had gone out, and the condemned man took off his prison uniform and put on the djellaba and the veil and the glasses and managed to escape by going out of the prison in the crowd of visitors.

"I came back home with the man's prison clothes, stuffed them into a floor cushion, and sewed a cover around it. I was startled every time I saw someone sit on it, and I found myself often looking at it in a puzzled way—why, I don't know.

"Anyway, the Sultan came back from exile and was welcomed as King Mohammed V; I gave birth to Souad; and your father came out of prison. Then the king gave him the document that appointed him mayor of Beni Mellal. We slaughtered a sheep on the occasion of Souad's naming party in Casablanca. My friend Fatna's husband, bless his soul, said, 'We won't eat until we hear the announcement of Si Hmed's appointment on the news bulletin.'

"While we were celebrating Souad's naming in Casablanca, Beni Mellal was welcoming your father with flowers, dates, milk, music, dancing, ululations, and lots of flags.

"Your uncle's wife Rabha says that while your father was being fêted, she happened to look up at the roof of one of the houses and saw some jars there, blackened with smoke, hanging upside down. 'I knew that was the evil work of the former mayor's family,' she said. Witchcraft against your father. So she pointed up and shouted, 'Look!' Look at that!' And people in the crowd picked up stones and threw them at the jars and broke them into pieces."

"When will God rid Morocco of witchcraft?" I interrupted.

But my mother did not answer. She went on, "It was then that the Nasrani of El Ksiba, before he left for France, told your father, 'I do not blame you and I hope that you will not blame me. You were defending the interests of your country and I was defending the interests of mine.'"

"How moving!" I said sarcastically. "Defending his right to colonize and exploit! That's how a great power explains its interventions over the globe: 'Self interest.' 'American way of life.' Some people are not embarrassed to build their prosperity on the misery of others. Don't you see how they control Arab resources, and are even ready to shed blood for it? How would they like it if we could speak of protecting our interests in their region?"

My mother laughed and said, "You mean if we said, 'We have to insure access to your wheat,' for instance? Self-interest, eh? May Allah the Almighty grant us all equity in this unfair world!"

Then she went on. "When your father arrived in Beni Mellal, Caid Haddou sent for Robio and told him, 'Go to Si Hmed. Tell him that I want to give him my daughter in marriage. Tell him that I offer him a house as well, and a car, to reward him for what he did for the nation.' And when Robio relayed this message, your father said to him, 'Go back and ask him what about my wife? Didn't *she* do something for the nation as well? Is that how he wants to reward her?' Robio delivered the message and Caid Haddou sent him back with another message: 'Save that wife for the kitchen. My daughter is a modern woman and you can present her to mayors and caids.' Then your father sent Robio back again with this message: 'Yes, I will keep my wife for kitchen work but I already have modern women to present to caids and mayors. I have my daughters Leila and Fatiha.'"

My mother's voice would quaver at this point, and she would wipe her eyes with a shaking hand. "The people of Beni Mellal heard the story and someone composed a song about it. We moved there and one day Robio came to me with a pair of mountain partridges. 'What's this?' I asked, and he replied, 'The former police officer was hunting and he brought these for you.' I took them and put them in the refrigerator. I was puzzled. It turned out it was the same Moroccan police officer who came to me at the gate of the prison in Rabat and said, 'That husband of yours is a worthless bastard,' and then took me inside the prison and asked your father, 'Why are you against the Nasara? What have they done to you?'

"So Robio left, and then he came back and said, 'Give me a towel. That man washed his hands at the garden tap and he wants a towel.' I went along the dark corridor, and when I reached my bedroom door I saw the man through the French windows putting a bomb in the dirt and covering it with leaves. I went to Robio and said, 'Go with the man to his car and come back quickly.' When he came back I said to him, 'Go to Si Hmed in the office and tell him to come here at once! Run!' The office was not far.

"Robio ran off and I went to the end of the garden far from the house and stayed there. Your father came and I told him what I had seen the man doing. He went out and picked up the bomb and defused it, and I told him that the man had sent us a pair of partridges. 'Bring them to me,' he ordered. I brought them and he gave them to a dog. After the poor dog ate the birds, it died on the spot from the poison that was intended for us. And we lived to see that police officer die like a dog, and the people of Beni Mellal refuse to walk behind his funeral procession."

Chapter IV
RABAT

When my father became the mayor of Beni Mellal, we went to live outside the town in the house that had formerly belonged to the French contrôleur général. It had French windows, and flowering shrubs covered the outside walls with blossoms. It had a front garden and a back garden, each with a large lawn and flowers, all irrigated by small canals. The house stood on a cliff and was frightening at night, for a Muslim graveyard lay at the bottom of the cliff and scores of frogs croaked there after dark. Still, the house had a carnival atmosphere. We cooked day and night, and my mother's and my father's families came and went, as well as a succession of men and women visitors from Casablanca and Rabat.

At the beginning of the school year after Independence, my mother and Moulay Hmed, our driver, took me and Fatiha some three hundred kilometers away to Rabat, to the house of Haj Outhman Jorio. Haj Outhman had been a nationalist and was now supervisor of the most prestigious Arabic private school in Rabat. My father had asked Haj Outhman to enroll us at another, no-less-prestigious private school called M'hammed Guessous, because this school gave equal emphasis to the teaching of Arabic and French. Colonialism had ended and French was no longer imposed upon us, but my father had decided that we should learn it anyway, because facility in that language had acquired another significance: it meant knowledge of a European language—and that, my father believed, was important.

So it was that we were enrolled in a boarding school. Our French instructors were Algerians and our Arabic instructors were natives of Rabat. The day pupils were from Rabat, but the girls in the dormitory were daughters of wealthy Moroccan farmers, of important merchants from the Souss region of southern Morocco, and of dignitaries from all over the country. One year, the daughters of a Moroccan circus director joined us for a month or so, while the circus was touring the country. They climbed trees with great agility and provided us with amazing acrobatic performances on weekends.

From the very beginning my inclination towards Arabic was obvious. I excelled in it. I don't know whether I excelled because I loved it, or loved it because I excelled. Whichever it was, I started spending much of my time reading—perhaps also partly to forget my separation from my mother, which was painful.

Our Arabic instructor, Mr. Oufir, had built up a little Arabic library for us in a closet at the back of the classroom. Each one of us contributed one or two books to it. We borrowed each book for a small sum and the money was used to buy more books. I was, I think, the one who made the most use of that library. I was hungry for books and I read eagerly and widely, always in Arabic. This led me to become the boarding school's storyteller. On Sundays, if the weather was bad, the matron, a young Algerian woman called Badra, would take us all to the classroom, not to study but so that I could tell stories to the class. She would sit me down at her desk, then go to the back of the classroom and listen attentively. When I finished she would say to me, "You'll be a teacher." This prediction was later repeated by a woman who worked as a maid at the home of one of my friends. She said she saw in the cards that I would teach. Another speculation about my future occupation was made by Si Moukhtar, my aunt Hachmia's husband, who, whenever he heard me asking my grandmother endless questions, used to say, "Do you want to be a journalist, or what?"

I did not care what I might grow up to be. My only interest was in finding yet more books to read. The girls at the boarding school continued to ask me for new stories. They would sit around me on the ground in the courtyard, in a circle that grew wider and wider, with not a single space left. I exhausted the resources of our little classroom library. Then a school supervisor in Beni Mellal, who was a friend of my father's and admired my letters to him, sent me a fascinating volume of children's literature. This volume contained wonderful stories and beautiful pictures such as only Lebanese publishers knew how to produce. It was as huge as *A Thousand and One Nights* in the eyes of an Arab, or as big as the New York City telephone directory appears to an American. By the time I graduated from that school, I had read all of it over and over again.

Toward the end of that first year, I fasted during Ramadan for the first time. However, I had to go into the dining room at breakfast and lunch times because the woman in charge of meals prohibited fasting. She was a tough, heavy Algerian who looked to me rather like a prison guard. After several days, when she noticed that I was not eating; she came over to me and said, "Eat!"

"I'm fasting," I said.

"How can you fast, when I don't, and I'm as old as your mother?"

"I've reached puberty."

"You've what? If you don't eat I'll lock you up in your room. Fasting for a growing child?"

"Christian logic," I thought. "God knows better. If it were harmful for a child who has reached puberty, He wouldn't have required it. She is a Muslim but she thinks with a Christian mind." I was determined to resist and defend my faith no matter what, and I did so. Had not the Christian rule been done away with?

At the end of that first year at the boarding school, summer vacation arrived and Moulay Hmed came and drove us home. We got to Tadla and crossed Oum el-Rabia at the bridge where the current once took away our basket. But then the car headed toward El Ksiba instead of continuing on the road to Beni Mellal. We shouted, "It's the other way!"

"I know," Moulay Hmed said. "I have a surprise for you."

The familiar low white wall of our earlier childhood appeared, then the pine trees, the fort, the administration building, the French officers' mansions. The car reached the grounds of the El Ksiba controleur général's house, slowed down and passed through the gate.

"The controleur général's house?" we asked in disbelief.

"*Your* house," he answered.

This was the house where I had gone with some girls to peek in and see what a Christian party looked like; that was when my father hit me. Now this was our house. My father had been promoted to the position of the head caid in El Ksiba, which meant that he was the chief executive in charge of the whole district. Thus the residence of the former controleur général had been given to us. The car went up the driveway and the house appeared, majestic, white, with balconies. Next to it stood the guest house with a gabled red-tile roof and an old bougainvillea climbing up to the top, where it exploded in sumptuous scarlet blooms. Beside the guest house was the garage.

This mansion was just as extensive and beautiful as the one where we had lived in Beni Mellal. The front garden had a green lawn shaded by a huge willow tree, an ornamental pool amidst flowers, and a wooden trellis supporting a blossoming vine. A table and chairs stood inside, under the trellis. Bordering this garden on one side was a white wall; down below the wall lay the pine woods where we had played in our early childhood, and not far away the mountain was visible.

Behind the house was the stable, a fenced area holding a gazelle, and a barn with wood stacked up for winter. The house itself had six rooms. We kept everything as we found it except for the women's and men's rooms, which we redecorated in Moroccan style. The French had left all the furnishings, even the china and silverware.

My mother told us that in that house the remains of the national hero Hansali were prepared after having been moved from their previous grave. (It turned out that her information was incorrect, but it was a good story and we listened eagerly.) He was, as she used to relate, "an ordinary Berber shepherd in El Ksiba who had sworn an oath not to leave one Nasrani alive in that area. He had no weapons until he managed to steal a gun, and from a hiding place on the mountain he moved around secretly looking for French to shoot.

"The Nasrani of El Ksiba posted a reward for anyone who could bring news about the fugitive Hansali. Hansali remained in hiding until he could no longer endure his hunger. Then, carrying the gun on his back under his long robe, he went to the tent of some nomads and said, 'A guest of God.' 'Welcome!' they replied. But when he sat down the gun stuck out, and the tent owner winked to another fellow who then went out and informed the nearest military center. Soldiers came and arrested Hansali. He had killed I don't know how many Nasara and the whole army in the region was after him.

"They tortured Hansali, executed him, and threw his body in a hole. After Independence, when your father was appointed the head caid in El Ksiba, the crown prince Moulay al-Hassan and a group of nationalists came from Rabat and Casablanca and dug up his remains and washed them in the Islamic tradition. When they reburied him, there was a great procession attended by Moulay al-Hassan and some ministers, as well as a huge crowd praying for the Prophet.

"When they dug the hole where Hansali's body had been thrown, they found the remains of four other bodies."

We spent our vacations in that house and we were happy there. But whenever time came for us to make the return journey to Rabat, we became more and more distressed. By the time we had passed through Rabat's orange orchards and reached Victor Hugo Avenue, where the school was located, we were very upset.

Once when we were home in El Ksiba, a friend of my father's who worked in a gas station in Beni Mellal said that his wife had invited Fatiha and me to lunch. My father had friends from all walks of life, dignitaries as well as ordinary people. He considered them all a social resource by means of which he maintained contact with his own grassroots culture. So we had gone to the couple's little two-room house in Beni Mellal, and found there an older woman with short hair wearing expensive European dress. Shortly after we returned to school in Rabat, I was summoned to the reception room because, I was told, I had a visitor. There sat that same woman. She had come all the way from Beni Mellal with a present for me. In a tiny box was a ruby on a gold chain. When my father visited us I told him about it and he became furious. "Give it to me," he said. "I'll send it right back to her."

After that, whenever I went back home I would hear the story of my returned gift, always linked with the name of that older woman who, it seemed, had an extremely bad reputation in Beni Mellal.

83

It was around that time that things took a bad turn in our family. I was awakened one morning at school to hear that my parents and younger sisters had moved to Rabat. By this time Fatiha had begun to live at home, though I remained in the boarding school. After that when I went home on weekends, I always heard my mother complaining about the old black maid who had come with her from El Ksiba, or about some woman's belt she had found in the bedroom after she came back from a trip. I often found her crying, and when I asked why, someone would always say, "He's going to repudiate her." "He said he'll repudiate." Every time these words were pronounced her tears increased, until I came home one weekend and my father was not there.

The left-wing government, in which he was a member of the prime minister's cabinet, was no longer in power and my mother said that he had gone to Casablanca to be with that wicked woman, the "ruby woman." He went away without repudiating my mother and left our family in Rabat. I had to leave the boarding school. We had to leave the house and move to a modest apartment similar to the one where we had lived in Casablanca.

We felt totally abandoned, even though our father sent money for our family expenses with a driver who came late at night when he brought the socialist party newspaper to be distributed in Rabat. Then the money stopped when my father was arrested along with the leaders and members of the Union Nationale des Forces Populaires (UNFP), the opposition party, who were accused in the conspiracy against the monarchy, known as "The Plot of 1963."

So we began to walk to a different school. I entered ninth grade and Fatiha eighth in the Moulay Youssef Boys' High School. This school was chosen because it was the only place in Rabat where the *Lettres Originelles*, a new academic discipline, was taught. I was still hungry for Arabic literature; it was the only subject that could satisfy my craving for learning.

In Moulay Youssef's program of *Lettres Modernes* we were taught some subjects in French and some in Arabic. In French we had language and literature, geography, history, and the sciences. In Arabic we had language and literature, philosophy, and eight hours a week of the Qur'an, the Hadith, Islamic jurisprudence and the foundations of Islamic religion. We had one instructor for literary Arabic and another for religious matters. Both men were graduates of the Qarawiyin, the famous theological university in Fez, founded in 933 A.D... In fact, by the time we finished the four-year program under these men's tutelage we had completed the equivalent of the Qarawiyin B.A. in Islamic theology.

One of these two instructors was Professor Moulay Ali Alaoui, who would later, in the 1990s, become a well-known member of parliament. Professor Alaoui was unique in both his manner and his approach to his academic subject matter. We had never before experienced any instructor like him. In Moroccan culture we expect an instructor to be haughty and severe, to erect a barrier between himself and his students. He should be a person in whose presence the student freezes with awe, palms moist, throat dry and yet trembling like a leaf in the wind. We traditionally regard a school instructor as a master of a craft, a man of authority who holds absolute power while he pours information into the student, using an antiquated method of rote memorization: "So-and-so says...," "So-and-so thinks...," "So-and-so interprets..." Thus the student must read the text through the opinions of all those so-and-so's rather than from his or her own point of view. Students are expected to open their eyes and ears and shut their mouths. This is why highly educated Moroccans are often poor orators. One has only to hear the speeches of Moroccan ministers of state and members of parliament, or the statements of speakers on radio and television panels, to realize that Moroccan rhetoric is typically inferior to that of peers in other Arab and Western countries—whose addresses are so often a delight to the mind, the ear and the emotions.

The teaching method used by Professor Alaoui, however, was for us a welcome deviation from that antiquated system. He was a pedagogue in the best sense of the word, with a natural talent for teaching. God had put in him the knowledge of modern education, and had put him in our path, to open for us during those four years the gates to the gardens and treasures of Arabic that are contained in the Qur'an and the Hadith. Later I was to find his wonderful style in universities in the United States, where education emphasizes the development of the student's faculties of opinion and expression, not rote memorization. There, as with Professor Alaoui, telling the student, "Wrong!" instead of "Right, but there is another way to interpret that," and correcting with a red pen instead of a light pencil are considered forms of psychological aggression and oppression that might prevent the student from voicing or writing his or her own ideas.

After all, an instructor is a human being, not a despot; he or she is made humble before God and in the minds of other people because of knowledge. An instructor should gain respect through affection, not fear, I believe.

We were studying canonical books, and yet Professor Alaoui allowed us to express our opinions, and we respected him with affection and even a sense of fellowship. We spoke up and discussed the texts in a healthy, comfortable atmosphere. The closeness of our relationship sometimes led us into friendly conspiracies with him. Because we usually finished our courses before the end of the term, and because he was very busy with the newspaper of his political party, he sometimes told us at the beginning of breaks between classes, "I'm going out. I've something to do. Let me go first, then you may leave one by one."

We sometimes got into heated political discussions with Professor Alaoui. These sessions were in themselves classes in self-expression, even though they had a tendency to resemble meaningless party speeches. Our arguments clearly reflected the discourse of the UNFP newspaper, with clichés such as "feudal policy," "police dictatorship," "absolute power," "despotic power," "police power," "feudal system," "reactionary authorities," "agents of colonialism," "agents of the system," "proletariat," "democracy," "demagogy," and all the rest of the terminology of the opposition movement's political dictionary. We were too young to understand most of these phrases, but we repeated them like parrots.

That mind-set was natural, at least as far as I was concerned, considering that I was intellectually influenced by my father—and also that my father was in the hands of the police, the archenemy of the opposition in that day—but I do not know what made the other students take the same position and use the same language. Were their fathers also members of the UNFP? Or was it only because the words "opposition" and "socialism" fascinated the Moroccan youth of that period?

We were politicized little beings who debated in the style of third-world opposition movements. We demanded the right to speak, snatched it, and when we got it we refused to give it back. We talked and talked and talked and refused to listen. It was a democracy that served our own interests, in precisely the same way that American democracy is fueled by self-interest.

I say that now, of course, as I look back on that strange classroom. We, the members of the opposition, who claimed we wanted to establish equity and democracy, actually took away the right to speak from our adversary—represented in that setting by our instructor, Professor Alaoui. We discarded his opinions and believed that democracy meant that our opinion must prevail, because we knew the Truth. I do not remember ever having listened to an opposing point of view in those days.

By then I had visited my father for the first time in Kenitra prison, where he was being held. I did not understand how a person who had gone to prison for the cause of Independence when the country was under colonial rule could then go to prison again *after* it had won Independence from such rule and the colonizers had departed. True, I was imbued with a lot of preconceived ideas that I did not really understand, but I believed that a person in a position of power over another did not have the right to torture his opponent, no matter what the offense might be. I thought that such a person ought to reflect: suppose our positions were reversed, my ideas would "logically" be the wrong ones. Would my opponent then have the right to torture me? No, he would not. This reasoning confirmed my belief that it is never justifiable for one human being to torture another.

On my first visit to my father in Kenitra prison, I saw that part of my father's face had been smashed like a tin plate hit by a piece of iron. I did not know what method of torture could do that, nor did I talk to anyone about it, and the question has stayed with me all these years. I was certainly politicized, but I was also young and naive, and I had not learned from life yet. Across the two wire fences I asked my father, "Do you want a radio?"

The guard in his dark uniform burst into a horselaugh and said, "I suppose you want to get him a TV set, too!" (Of course, both radios and television sets were forbidden in prison.)

My father smiled at the man's crude assumption that his prisoners wished only to please. But I sensed that my father's smile was tinged with fear, the same fear that I was to see again, years later, on that day at Casablanca's Anfa Airport, when he walked backward in front of another rude policeman and tried to shut me up with an awkward movement of his hand. How had he been able to stand up to the French police under torture, I wondered, only to fear now one of his own countrymen wearing a uniform of authority? What had they done to him?

It is true that the UNFP members were obstinate, flamboyant, and aggressive and these qualities came across in their words as well as actions. The clichés that my classmates and I parroted were used in UNFP members' homes and meetings and were published by their newspaper, which was sold in broad daylight. Many of these men and women were young, elated by their nation's victory over France, mesmerized by mainstream ideology, and uncaring about the consequences of their conduct. In the first years after Independence, they thought they would be protected by their record as active nationalists. They took credit for bringing Independence to Morocco, and therefore considered it their right to practice that Independence by running the government and implementing their own ideas. They had believed that public opinion, represented by young people, workers, peasants, and the educated elite, was behind them. When they realized, from the results of communal and parliamentary elections, that they did not have as much popular support as they thought, they lost patience and might have actually planned the so-called Plot of 1963. After their policies were rejected, they began, out of disappointment and a sense of betrayal, to insult the system and to qualify it with negative attributes such as those parroted by me and my classmates at Moulay Youssef.

When they boycotted the communal elections, the UNFP members wrote in their newspaper things like "horsemen were brought into the Marrakech district to shoot their guns in the air in order to attract the public to the polling stations," and that the authorities in the Asafi district "announced the good news that mint tea was being served inside the polls," and that "the tone of the town criers has changed; they are now saying that he who does not vote will be charged a penalty." They also wrote, "The anniversary of August 20 (the date on which the French had exiled Mohammed V) was commemorated in the compound of the royal palace, as usual, without the real heroes of liberation, and indeed in the presence of a number of traitors, proponents of feudalism and advocates of old and new colonialism. These are the very traitors whom the resistance condemned in the name of the people, and who escaped being sentenced either by chance or because of the protection of the French army and police." They wrote, "The merciless and illogical way in which the faithful nationalists are dealt with today can raise in the citizens near-certainty that the present policy is a continuation of that of the Protectorate, which loathed the nationalists and plotted against them. Do not the continuing detentions and oppressions make us think of what the French Résidents did when they were ruling Morocco? Fighting ideas with force does not and cannot succeed."

The writers at the UNFP newspaper compared their country with another that had been under French rule: "The government of Algeria believes in socialism and the government of Morocco centers itself on feudalism. It is only one year since Algeria won its independence, yet our brother country is already ahead of Morocco, which won its independence eight years ago. Algeria has solved the problem of land ownership to the benefit of the peasants. It has nationalized companies, enterprises, factories, institutions, and has employed citizens in them. It has introduced plans for agriculture, industrialization, literacy, building villages, and taking care of those who fought in the resistance. In the province of Oran it has nationalized over 5,000 hectares of the lands of colonists and put under the control of the supervising agricultural committees an additional 8,000 hectares. It has nationalized some important factories such as the brick factory, the plaster factory, the pasta factory, and the Oran wood factory. It has also built about 400 homes."

On the other hand, the members of the UNFP used the newspaper as a forum for criticizing a Moroccan government decree about agricultural reform and the recovery of the lands of the colonists. Why? Because the reform was to be implemented in stages, and because it dealt with only 270,000 hectares of the lands of the colonists and guaranteed property rights to the remaining 700,000 hectares to original owners. They objected because the Moroccan government decree gave compensation to the French, even for the lands of colonists, which would cost the country billions. According to the UNFP newspaper, this decree was the "agricultural reform that the government of Morocco wants to apply under the supervision of the French government." It was called "false agricultural reform" and "plan of absolute power." "It would take eight years to recover all the lands," but "in Algeria only two years." "Moreover, the outrageous raise in the price of sugar announced by the government will have disastrous repercussions on the standard of living in Morocco and the standard of prices, and will affect every branch of the economy..." Furthermore, they added, "The compensation fund was not used properly. This raise in the price of sugar is a tax imposed on the laboring class, poor peasants and people with small incomes, instead of imposing a direct tax on those who make huge profits."

The Moroccan opposition was having a honeymoon with Algeria. Its members looked at that country with approving eyes and saw revolutionary achievements in any action it undertook, however banal—the nationalization of the pasta factory, for example, as if nationalizing a pasta factory represented immense progress in the brother state. On the other hand, they looked for mistakes in the Moroccan system and inflated the significance of those mistakes—such as the rise in the price of sugar—making readers of the newspaper believe that Morocco was going back to the Year of Hunger. And the same treatment was given to other matters such as "the disaster of education," which "includes no more than 50 percent of the children, a great number of whom are dropping out of school." The UNFP newspaper continued to publish, despite police efforts to burn down the offices, and despite the number of party members, like my father, who were jailed in 1963 for "plotting" against the system.

Years later I asked my mother, "What can you tell me about father's detention in the "plot" charge?"
"Nothing."
"How did you hear the news of his arrest?"
"I don't know."
"What do you remember obout that period?"
"Nothing."
Is it not strange that events of that magnitude could be wiped out of my mother's memory? Strange that she could not or would not tell me about them? But I remember that when the trial started, each morning we planted ourselves at the iron gate of the Court of Appeals in Rabat and at the end of each day my mother would bring back to our

apartment the prisoners' wives who came from Casablanca and had nowhere to stay. Thus, news about the trial was transferred to our apartment and discussion about what was happening continued late into the night.

"There's no plot. The idea of a plot has been fabricated by the establishment against the UNFP. When they were arrested they were at a meeting to study the situation in the interior and decide what position to take concerning the forged communal elections."

"Yes, there is a plot! They say it is not exactly a plot but a continuation of liberation."

"The Minister of the Interior told the representative of French radio and TV that the meeting was held to organize revolution all over Morocco."

"That's why the police are asking, 'Who are the members of the secret organization?' and 'Who are the members of the secret cell?' and 'Where do they meet?' and 'Where are the arms?' and 'Where are you hiding them?'"

"The authorities want to force them to admit their guilt and to say the accusation is true. That's why they beat them and use electricity, water, and salt, and all those methods they learned from the French secret service. That's why they've refused to allow in court the lawyers sent by the French socialists. The government doesn't want the foreigners to see the marks of torture."

"Banini, the minister of the interior, told the French lawyers, 'The government will not accept your participation in the defense because you are not proficient in Arabic.' As if those people in the government, were proficient in it themselves!"

"Arabic! Then why do they reject the Arab lawyers from the socialist parties in Syria and Egypt?"

"France is going to protest the rejection of foreign lawyers and its press is criticizing the rejection. Even an important newspaper in New York wrote that King Hassan has started a campaign of oppression against the men who realized the independence of Morocco and reestablished the legitimate monarchy."

"France and America had better remember their own history. Didn't 300,000 blacks march on Washington after they couldn't take any more of American racism, segregation and tyranny?"

Eventually the French lawyers and the Arab lawyers departed, but the Moroccan lawyers stayed. The trial dissolved into turmoil and the Moroccan lawyers Abderrahim Bouabid and Mohammed Tbar were celebrated for their ingenious arguments and flamboyant performances on behalf of the accused.

One day my mother and my sisters and I came and waited as usual in the Court of Appeals, which is now the House of Parliament. The police kept us between iron barriers in the lobby of the main trial chamber, the chamber which is now known as the Moroccan Room. (The police always took their time before letting us enter the courtroom.)

Many years later I began working in the parliament, and on my very first day, the 29th of December, 1990, I found myself in exactly the same place where I had waited with my mother and my sisters to enter the courtroom when my father's trial was being held. But in 1990 I stood with Moroccans who were waiting to meet a delegation from the Congress of the United States. The delegation was on a survey trip to the Maghreb countries just before the Gulf War. Across twenty-seven years an image flashed into my mind in all its violence. On that earlier day that I remember with such clarity, there were many of us prisoners' families behind barriers in that lobby, and if the place had a memory it would have remembered me. I was first in line, standing very politely, when an emaciated young brown-skinned policeman pushed me aggressively for no apparent reason. I screamed and my scream reached the trial chamber and all the prisoners rose in protest. They cried out to the judge, "Look at the savage way the police are treating our children!"

It was clear and embarrassing proof that, if the police were abusing children in public courthouses, what they were doing to their fathers in the basements of their local police stations might be worse.

I could not understand why any person would behave in such an aggressive way toward someone who had done nothing, even if that person were a policeman in a newly independent country. I was appalled. A heavy, choking feeling built up in my breast and rose to my throat in bitterness. I withdrew from the barriers and walked with my sister Fatiha up Mohammed V Avenue towards the Sunni mosque. A policeman followed us. He was a short, heavy, very brown-skinned man, with cropped black hair, and his fleshy face had the roughness of sackcloth. He caught up with us and started walking beside us in heavy measured steps, throwing at us glances filled with hatred. Then he opened his mouth and said to me, "You bitch!"

Nobody had ever said such a thing to me before and it dumbfounded me, deepened my confusion and pain and my feeling of injustice, and threw me into dark despair. I had never been treated with such vulgar hostility by the police of France. Could this be our Moroccan police? And that face merged in my mind with the face of the district officer in Agdal, who had the same rustic look and decaying teeth. That was the man who had refused to give us the documents we needed long ago because of our father's political views.

Fatiha and I took refuge in the grounds of our school and sat on a low wall. The policeman with his fleshy face stood on the pavement outside and silently glared at us through the gate for what seemed like a long time. We looked back at him, I through my tears, which did not stop that day.

Sometime after that, it was reported to my mother that a prisoner's wife had said of her, "If I were Fettouma, I would not set foot inside the door of this court. Her husband's mistress is standing on one side, and she is standing on the other."

When I heard this gossip I said to my mother, "Clearly the camel doesn't see its hump. The cause of your trouble waits for your husband, just like you do, in the crowd at the entrance to the court. But how can that woman criticize *your* presence, when the woman who has taken her own husband sits with him openly in the seats of those who are accused? And what about that other prisoner who managed to insult the public prosecutor of the court by having sexual intercourse with his wife? What revolution and what struggle and what national interest does all this behavior serve? And now that you've heard with your own ears what people are saying, Mother, let's not visit him anymore, and please don't say, 'They're going to criticize me,' because nobody is going to criticize you."

For me, activists who do not care about morality are no different from their opponents. How can a person fight the state to establish what is right when one does not respect this concept in one's own family? What is the difference between a secular legal system and an "Islamic" one that rules with the laws of the West and feeds its budget with money obtained from taxes on the sale of wine and on gambling? According to the Qur'an, "Those who do not rule with the law of God are indeed the unjust." In another verse, such people are referred to as "the corrupt." What happened after Independence in Morocco was not a matter of right and wrong but rather a struggle for power. That is, of course, a conclusion I have reached only now, because I needed some time to pass before I could stand back from the situation and look at it in perspective.

My youngest uncle, Sidi Mohammed, said, "I'll go to your father and make him choose between that woman and us. I'll tell him, 'People are talking.' I'll tell him, 'We stand at the prison gate and they bring out your laundry and give it to that other woman, and at the front gate of the Court of Appeals we stand in one place and she stands in another with your brother Said.'"

He went to the prison and came back looking embarrassed.

"Well?" we asked.

"I told him, 'We won't visit you anymore if she goes on visiting you.'"

"What did he say?"

"Don't visit me."

For some time we were dismayed by this response and stopped visiting my father. But then the women from Casablanca who came in the evening to sleep in our apartment reported to us several times: "He was looking for you in the seats area." And our will broke and we went back to stand behind barriers. When he was released he came to see us on his way to Casablanca.

Later, in the early seventies, after his involvement with that other woman had ended, he started visiting us. I would get into heated debates with him, always about politics, and suggested that his behavior and that of some of his fellows in their private lives had shaken my confidence in the party as a whole. My mother would stand in the doorway motioning nervously to us to be quiet, and say, "Enough! People will think that you're arguing." And he'd say to her, "It's okay. This is a good thing."

In 1976 I came back from an Arab Youth Festival in Baghdad and told my father about an exchange of words I had had with a member of the Algerian delegation. This man was named Brahim Harran; he was a young assistant professor at the Faculté des Lettres in Algiers who held a position of responsibility in the Algerian National Youth Organization. This was when animosity between Morocco and Algeria on the issue of sovereignty over the Western Sahara was at its height. This man had said to me, "You have betrayed your father. How can you work for the prime minister when your father has such a strong record of opposition?"

When my father heard this, his mind reacted in its usual deductive and exploratory way, "No doubt he found out about me from the UNFP members in the Moroccan delegation," he said.

But I repeated to my father what I had said to that Algerian: "I told him, 'If the other side thought with the same logic—the logic of our neighborhood official in Agdal—then not a single son or daughter of anyone active in the opposition would ever work in our country.' I also told him, 'First, I am Moroccan and have the right to work in any Moroccan organization if I am qualified for the position. Isn't that the true spirit of democracy? Second, to be frank with you, I am amazed that my father has supported ideas such as those of the opposition. How could an intellectual, modern Muslim like my father have deserted eternal and basic principles that emanate from his nature, his roots, his culture, and his identity, principles that were formulated by God? How could he have adopted the secular principles imported from the West?'"

My father said nothing. He remained thoughtful and silent.
My father died in 1982. He was sixty three years old. I still have
no answers to the questions I asked him that day.

Printed and bound by CPI Group (UK) Ltd, Croydon, CR0 4YY

13/04/2025

14656493-0002